how2become

HOW TO BECOME A CIVIL ENFORCEMENT OFFICER

by Richard McMunn

Orders: Please contact How2become Ltd, Suite 3, 50 Churchill Square Business Centre, Kings Hill, Kent ME19 4YU.

You can also order via the e mail address info@how2become.co.uk.

ISBN:

First published 2014

Typeset for How2become Ltd by Anton Pshinka

Printed in Great Britain for How2become Ltd by CMP

WELCOME

Welcome to 'How 2 Become a Civil Enforcement Officer'. This guide has been designed to help you prepare for and pass the Civil Enforcement Officer (CEO) selection process.

The author of this guide, Richard McMunn, spent over 16 years in the UK Fire Service. He worked at many different fire stations at every position up to Station Manager, and he has also sat on numerous interview panels assessing potential candidates. You will find his advice invaluable and inspiring in your pursuit of this highly challenging yet rewarding career.

Whilst the selection process to join the Local Authority as a CEO is highly competitive, there are a number of things you can do in order to improve your chances of success, and they are all contained within this guide.

The guide itself has been split up into useful sections to make it easier for you to prepare for each stage. Read each section carefully and take notes as you progress. Don't ever give up on your dreams; if you really want to become a CEO then you can do it. The way to prepare for a job in the Local Authority, who will be your employer for this specific role, is to embark on a programme of 'in depth' preparation, and this guide will show you exactly how to do that.

If you need any help with motivation, getting fit or further interview help and advice, then we offer a wide range of products to assist you. These are all available through our online shop **www.how2become.com.**

Once again, thank you for your custom and we wish you every success in your pursuit to becoming a Civil Enforcement Officer.

Work hard, stay focused and be what you want…

Best wishes,

The how2become team

The How2become Team

Preface by author Richard McMunn

I joined the Fire Service on January the 25th 1993 after completing four years in the Fleet Air Arm branch of the Royal Navy. In the build up to joining the Fire Service I embarked on a comprehensive training programme that would see me pass the selection process with relative ease. The reason why I passed the selection process with ease was solely due to the preparation and hard work that I had put in during the build-up.

I have always been a great believer in preparation. Preparation was my key to success, and it is also yours. Without the right level of preparation you will be setting out on the route to failure. The role of CEO for any Local Authority is very hard to join, simply due to the level of competition you are likely to face, but if you follow the steps that I have compiled within this guide then you will increase your chances of success dramatically.

Remember, you are learning how to be a successful candidate, not a successful CEO – the training for the role will come later.

All Local Authorities have changed a great deal over the past few years, and even more so in how they assess potential candidates for internal positions such as the Civil Enforcement Officer. You will be assessed against your knowledge of the role and also with regards to your 'potential' for carrying out the job both competently and professionally. With these factors in mind, it is essential that you learn everything you can about the role you are applying for and also be able to provide evidence of where you meet the assessable competencies – more on these later!

Before you apply to join the Local Authority as a CEO, you need to be fully confident that you are capable of delivering an exceptional level of service to the public. If you think you can do it, and you can rise to the challenge, then you just might be the type of person the Local Authority are looking for.

As you progress through this guide you will notice that the qualities and competencies required to be a CEO are a common theme. You must learn these qualities, and also be able to demonstrate throughout the selection process that you can meet them, if you are to have any chance of successfully passing the selection process.

CONTENTS

CHAPTER 1

The role of a Civil Enforcement Officer and some frequently asked questions

THE ROLE OF A CIVIL ENFORCEMENT OFFICER AND SOME FREQUENTLY ASKED QUESTIONS

Civil Enforcement Officer (CEO) is the new name for Parking Attendants, or Traffic Wardens as they are often still called. The main aim of a CEO is to enforce legislation governed by Civil Law.

CEO's are employed by a Local Authority to enforce parking restrictions in their dedicated area in order to maintain a free flow of traffic, to help keep pedestrians safe and to also ensure that all parking requirements are being complied with. As a uniformed presence on the streets, they contribute towards the Local Authorities key aims and objectives. CEO's are provided with communications equipment which enables them to be in constant radio contact with community wardens, police community support officers and other members of the Local Authority team. Not only is this for Health and Safety reasons but it is also to aid in the Local Authorities aim of refusing crime and anti-social behaviour. Although a CEO's primary aim is to enforce parking restrictions within an area, they are also a useful pair of eyes and ears 'on the ground'.

CEO's issue parking tickets called Penalty Charge Notices (PCNs) to vehicles parked in contravention of the regulations under the Traffic Management Act 2004. PCNs may be issued on any day and at any time when the restriction is in force. Some restrictions, such as double yellow lines, remain in force 24 hours a day.

Although the typical working day will very much vary from authority to authority, most CEO's patrol the streets and the car parks 7 days a week, from 7am to 9pm. Despite common belief they do not work to targets or quotas but in order to achieve compliance with parking regulations, they are instructed to issue a penalty charge notice (PCN) whenever a vehicle is found to be in contravention of a parking restriction. They normally give an observation period to check whether loading is taking place or if the driver is in the vicinity at a pay and display machine, purchasing a ticket. However, certain contraventions, such as waiting on zig zag lines or in bus stop clearways, do not require an observation period and the penalty is usually issued instantly. If the driver has not returned following an observation period, the vehicle is checked for valid permits, tickets or notes and if necessary, a PCN is issued.

Once the PCN has been issued, photographs are taken as evidence of the vehicle in contravention and notes are made in the CEO's pocket book or hand held computer. Photographs are helpful in cases of a challenge but are not compulsory. In bad weather or if it is dark they are unlikely to be useful so the evidence mainly relied upon are the notes made at the time. No photographs are allowed to be taken if there are occupants in or around the vehicle.

If the driver returns whilst the PCN is being issued, it can be served upon the motorist instead of being fixed to the windscreen. Once issued, the CEO must not take back the PCN but will advise the motorist to follow the instructions on the PCN, or to contact the Parking Office for advice. The CEO does not have the authority to give opinions on the possible outcome of any challenge and is not obliged to stay at the scene if being verbally abused or threatened. All CEO's are equipped with radios and can call for assistance if necessary, either to help members of the public with their queries or to call for help if under threat. Any physical or verbal abuse of the CEO is recorded and if serious, will be reported to the Police by the Local Authority.

Frequently asked questions

Q What do CEO's do?

A civil enforcement officer is employed by local authorities or contractors to enforce parking regulations on public streets and car parks around towns and cities.

Q. How are appeals against parking tickets dealt with?

www.patrol-uk.info - This website provides information about the enforcement of parking tickets as well as parking and bus lane regulations for councils in England (outside London) and Wales that are in the Civil Enforcement Scheme.

Appeals against Parking or Moving Traffic tickets issued by London Councils or Transport for London are dealt with through the 'Parking and Traffic Appeals Service' and their website can be found at: www.patas.gov.uk

Q. What would my duties be?

You would be responsible for patrolling public streets and car parks to identify potential parking infringements and issue parking tickets. Other duties may include dealing with customer enquiries, monitoring CCTV, reporting suspected abandoned vehicles, reporting faulty or damaged equipment, and carrying out minor repairs or maintenance on equipment.

You will use equipment like hand held computers and printers, two-way radios and cameras.

Q. What skills do I need to apply?

- Communication skills
- Customer service skills
- Organisational skills
- Literacy skills
- IT skills
- Conflict management skills
- Knowledge of Government legislation

Q. What qualifications do I need?

There are no formal entry requirements to become a Civil Enforcement Officer.

However, you could complete a Level 2 Award for Civil Enforcement Officers or an NVQ Level 2 in Controlling Parking Areas to develop your skills.

Q. What does the selection process entail?

The selection process for becoming a Civil Enforcement Officer will vary from Authority to Authority; however, as a general guide it will consist of the following:

- Application form and screening
- Assessment centre to assess numeracy and literacy skills
- Interview
- Health assessment or questionnaire

Q. What's the salary like as a CEO and are there any opportunities for progression?

The salary for a CEO will normally vary from authority to authority. However the following diagram will give you a good indication as to the level of salary you can expect to achieve and the 3 different position levels you can aspire to.

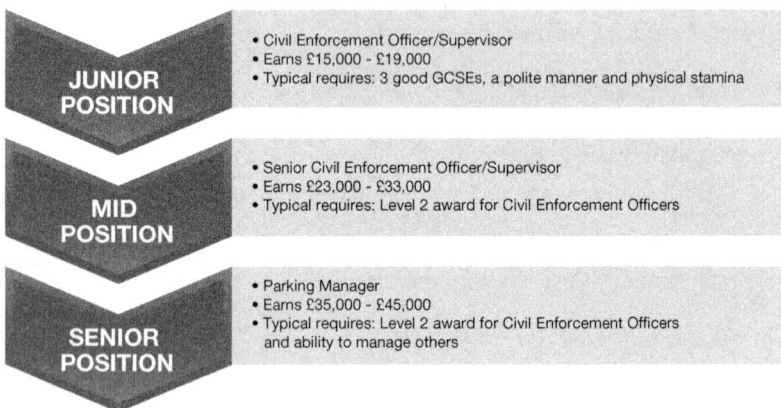

JUNIOR POSITION
- Civil Enforcement Officer/Supervisor
- Earns £15,000 - £19,000
- Typical requires: 3 good GCSEs, a polite manner and physical stamina

MID POSITION
- Senior Civil Enforcement Officer/Supervisor
- Earns £23,000 - £33,000
- Typical requires: Level 2 award for Civil Enforcement Officers

SENIOR POSITION
- Parking Manager
- Earns £35,000 - £45,000
- Typical requires: Level 2 award for Civil Enforcement Officers and ability to manage others

Q. Is there a standard approach used by Civil Enforcement Officer's?

Yes, the approach is defined in the Civil Enforcement Officer's Handbook. The local authority should produce a handbook for CEO's. This should be based on the training given to CEO's and could be used both as part of that training and as a guide to procedures for officers on duty. The handbook should explain the different types of parking contravention. Many authorities that already have civil parking enforcement powers, and service providers, have handbooks which can be used as a model. An authority could prepare a handbook alongside the specification for tenderers wishing to provide CEO services. Alternatively, an authority could require the contractor to provide a suitable handbook. The authority should check that the instructions in any handbook produced by a contractor comply with the law.

For London Boroughs, the Civil Enforcement Officers (CEO) handbook has been devised after general consultation with all Borough's to provide a standard approach to issuing Penalty Charge Notices (PCNs). Parking contraventions are dealt with by issuing a Penalty Charge Notice and, in appropriate circumstances, by clamping or removing the vehicle to a pound. The handbook provides guidance which has general relevance throughout a specific area. It is accepted that there will be local variations in policy and these will be a matter for each London Borough. CEO's will be instructed on how to deal with local variations. The handbook is intended as a reference document for use on-street or in the office. It describes the contraventions, their codes and details of information to be recorded in each case in order to prove that the contravention took place.

The handbook can be found by searching for 'Civil Enforcement Officer Handbook' online. It is advisable that you read it during your preparation for interview as you may be asked questions relating to its existence and content.

Q. When issuing a Parking Charge Notice (PCN), what information must be recorded by the CEO and shown on the PCN?

This information may vary depending on the Local Authority and the area; however, as a general guide the following essential information must be recorded:

1. Date the notice is served
2. Grounds of issue
3. Vehicle registration mark (VRM)

4. Date and time of alleged contravention

5. Contravention description and code (optionally with suffixes as appropriate)

6. Location of alleged contravention (street name).

Q. When issuing a Parking Charge Notice (PCN), is photographic evidence required?

Photographs should be taken whenever possible. Whilst they are not compulsory, the evidence provided is extremely useful. Photographs should be taken of:

1. The vehicle parked in contravention

2. The vehicle registration number

3. The dashboard showing the tax disc and any permits, vouchers or tickets

4. Any signs or time plates relating to the contravention

Now move on to the next section of the guide entitled 'top tips for passing the CEO selection process.

CHAPTER 2

Top tips for passing the CEO selection process

TOP TIPS FOR PASSING THE CEO SELECTION PROCESS

Having spent a lengthy amount of time working for a Local Authority, and having already sat on recruitment interview panels, I have noticed a number of common themes that have been applicable to those people who pass selection. I have called these common themes my top tips for success.

The following tips are worth their weight in gold and I strongly recommend you read them carefully and follow the action points provided at the end of each one. Although many will appear to be obvious, you would be amazed at how many people fail to take them on-board during their preparation and end up failing as a result!

TIP NUMBER 1 – PREPARATION, PREPARATION, PREPARATION

Preparation is the key to your success.

You must be prepared for every stage of the selection process and do everything you can to increase your chances of succeeding.

Find out when the Local Authority you want to join are recruiting for CEO's next and begin to prepare months in advance. You can sign up for **CEO job alerts** to be notified as soon as any Civil Enforcement Jobs become available in your area at the website **www.how2become.com.**

With regards to preparing for the selection process my biggest piece of advice is to get a copy of the person specification and the job description for the role and start to study the qualities and competencies required to perform the role professionally. You should also ensure that you can provide evidence of where you meet every assessable quality that is contained within the job description. For example, if one of the assessable qualities on the job description is that of 'conflict management', you must think of a previous work related situation you have been in before where you have demonstrated this skill. Anybody can attend an interview and tell the panel that they are good at managing conflict; however, providing real evidence of where you have previously managed conflict is an entirely different thing.

As the guide progresses I will cover preparation in more detail in order to give you every possible chance of succeeding.

Action points

Your key preparation areas should include the following:

- Learn and understand the qualities and skills required to become a Civil Enforcement Officer.
- Prepare to submit an outstanding application form which focuses on meeting the minimum assessable criteria.
- Spend some time working on, and improving, your physical fitness. As a CEO you will walk many miles each day and you need to demonstrate that you are capable of achieving this.
- Prepare for the assessment centre tests by working on your literacy skills. We have provided some sample tests for you within this guide but you may also decide to purchase some additional preparation/testing resources via our website www.how2become. com.
- Work on your interview technique and prepare answers to the interview questions contained within this guide.

TIP NUMBER 2 – BE PHYSICALLY AND MENTALLY FIT

Make sure that you are both physically and mentally fit.

Whilst you will not directly be assessed against your physical fitness during the selection process it is vital that you are able to demonstrate to the employer that you are physically fit and capable of meeting the demands of the role. As I stated earlier, as a CEO you will be walking many miles a day, which will certainly keep your fitness levels up anyway!

During your preparation it may be worth considering changing your diet to make sure that you are eating the correct foods. Make sure you eat foods that will give you energy and also those that contain the right vitamins to ensure you are at your best. If you think you are overweight then the best form of exercise to take in order to lose weight is walking at a brisk pace every day for at least 20 minutes. Walking is also a great way to prepare yourself for the role of a CEO and it will also mean you can hit the ground running once you start your new job. You'll be amazed at the difference you feel in just a few weeks after you start your walking regularly!

In relation to your mental fitness, cut out alcohol and caffeine in the weeks leading up to your assessment and interview. Drink plenty of water and try to eat your 5 portions of fruit and vegetables every day. Again, you will be amazed at how much energy you gain simply by looking after yourself.

Depending on your current level of fitness, I would advise that you spend approximately 25% of your total preparation time on improving your fitness levels.

Action points

- Embark on a structured fitness programme that is designed to help you improve your fitness. You do not need to be very fit to become a CEO; however, it is my advice that you improve your fitness levels to meet the demands of the role if you feel you are currently not up to standard. We have provided you with a free Civil Enforcement Officer fitness guide towards the end of this book which will help you with your preparation.
- Drink plenty of water in the build up to the assessment and interview.
- Cut out alcohol and caffeine during your preparation.
- Eat healthily.

TIP 3 – LEARN THE CIVIL ENFORCEMENT OFFICER'S ROLE

Learn everything there is to know about the CEO's role.

Get hold of the job description and person specification for the role and study the content, making sure you understand what it involves.

An almost guaranteed question at the interview stage will be "Tell us what you know about the role of a CEO?" Your answer should reflect that you have gone out of your way to learn about the role and that you understand what it now involves. Many candidates will tell the interview panel that the job is 'all about making money for the Council through issuing parking tickets". This couldn't be further from the truth. The role involves enforcing parking restrictions to ensure the safety of the roads, the safety of pedestrians and also the safety of all road users. If we didn't employ CEO's, the roads would be chaos and most unsafe!

Those candidates who successfully pass the Civil Enforcement Officer selection process are able to demonstrate an in depth knowledge and understanding of the role throughout selection. Read the person specification and job description chapter from this guide carefully and you will start to understand the role more clearly.

Action points

- Obtain a copy of the job description and also the person specification that are required to perform the role competently. Read them both carefully and understand what the job entails.

- Be able to match your own skills and experiences with the personal qualities. This is great preparation for the application form and the interview stages.

- Visit and study the website of the Local Authority you are applying to join and in particular forces on the parking services section. This will tell you more about the role of a CEO and also the role the Local Authority plays in aiming to reduce parking offences within its areas of responsibility.

TIP 4 – VISIT THE LOCAL AUTHORITIES PARKING SERVICES OFFICES

In order to gain a thorough understanding of the role and what is involved, my advice would be to make contact with the local parking services office through the Local Authority website you are applying to join and request a visit in order to learn about the role you are applying for. Of course, the parking services officer may decline your request for a familiarisation visit; however, the worst that can happen is they say no. The likelihood is however, they will say yes, and you will be permitted to make a short visit to the parking services office in order to try and learn more about the role of a CEO and what they do on a day-to-day basis.

Here's a sample letter/email you can use when contacting the local Parking Services office manager to try and arrange a familiarisation visit:

SAMPLE LETTER/EMAIL

Mr Richard McMunn,
31, Fictitious Street,
Fictown,
Ficton
FCT 1AW

Dear Sir/Madam,

RE: Civil Enforcement Officer vacancy

I have recently applied to become a Civil Enforcement Officer within your department of the Local Authority and have been working hard to improve my knowledge and understanding of the role. To that end, I am writing to ask for permission to arrange a short familiarisation visit to the Parking Services Office in order to learn more about the role of a CEO, what it entails and the work that is carried out by the team within the office. This will help me during my preparation for the role and also help me to gain a thorough understanding of the good work you carry out at the Local Authority in order to enforce parking restrictions.

I fully appreciate that you are very busy but would be extremely grateful if you would allow me the opportunity to visit the office. Thank you for your time.

Yours faithfully,

Richard McMunn

Richard McMunn
Tel: 07890 183 XXX
Email: richardmcmunn@email.com

Action points

- Visit the Parking Services section of the Local Authority website and learn as much information as possible about the type of work they undertake.
- Make contact with the Parking Services Office at the Local Authority and attempt to arrange a familiarisation visit once you apply.

TIP NUMBER 5 – UNDERSTAND AND BELIEVE IN EQUALITY AND FAIRNESS

Equality and Fairness plays a big part within any Local Authority.

How we treat people at work, regardless of their sex, religious beliefs, age, sexual orientation or background etc. is extremely important. You must ensure that you understand what Equality and Fairness means and the principles behind it. More importantly, you need to believe in it.

The Local Authority wants to employ people who are capable of not just following their policies and procedures, but believing in them too. Nobody wants to go to work and be either bullied or treated inappropriately and you must be capable of treating everyone at work, and in society, with respect and dignity.

> *"Equality is not about treating everybody the same, but recognising we are all individuals, unique in our own way. Equality and fairness is about recognising, accepting and valuing people's unique individuality according to their needs. This often means that individuals may be treated appropriately, yet fairly, based on their needs."*

I also advise that you try to find out a little bit about the Equality and Fairness policies that are used by the Local Authority you are applying to join. Whilst this is not essential, it will ensure you understand what is expected of you as a Civil Enforcement Officer within your chosen Local Authority.

Once again, this can usually be done by visiting the Local Authorities website.

Action points

- Understand and believe in Equality and Fairness.
- Whilst not essential, try to obtain a copy of the equality policy. Read it, and try to understand what the Local Authority expects from its employees.

TIP NUMBER 6 – CONSIDER COMPLETING A LEVEL 2 AWARD FOR CIVIL ENFORCEMENT OFFICERS OR AN NVQ LEVEL 2 IN CONTROLLING PARKING AREAS

I must stress that completing a level 2 award for Civil Enforcement Officer's or obtaining an NVQ level 2 in controlling parking areas is not essential, simply because some Local Authorities may offer you this training as part of your development once you become successful. However, whilst not essential, obtaining one of these qualifications prior to application might work in your favour. Picture the scene there are 3 CEO vacancies available with a Local Authority and there are 10 candidates on the shortlist who have successfully passed the application form stage, assessment centre and interviews. Out of the 10 candidates you are the only one who has gained a level 2 award for civil enforcement officers. Your chances of being chosen as one of the successful 3 will greatly increase.

The level 2 award for Civil Enforcement Officer's qualification will enable you to learn, develop and practise the essential skills needed to work as a parking enforcement officer. It recognises your professional ability and will help you to progress in your career. This qualification has been developed specifically for those working, or wishing to work, as Parking Enforcement Officers.

To find out more about this course and the different companies which offer it, please visit **www.cityandguilds.com**

TIP NUMBER 7 – CARRY OUT COMMUNITY WORK

Although not essential, it would be beneficial if you can demonstrate that you are, or have been involved, in some form of community work.

The role of a CEO is very much about working with the local community and if you can demonstrate you are capable of this, you will have an advantage. This may be in the form of local charity work or helping out with your local Scout group etc. The options are endless but at the end of the day you will be able to demonstrate on your application form that you are willing and capable of working with the local community.

You may be asked during the interview if you have been involved in any community work, so it will be good if you have had that experience.

If you have not had any experience of any such work then it is never too late to begin. Why not carry out a sponsored swim, cycle ride or car wash and donate the money to a local charity? If you play team sports then you could arrange a charity game and donate the money to good causes.

You need to stand out from the competition during the application stage and this could be a good way to achieve that. If I was sat on an interview panel and a candidate had carried out some form of community work then I would be impressed!

Action point

- Consider carrying out some form of community/charity work.

TIP NUMBER 8 – WRITTEN TEST PREPARATION

You would be amazed at how many candidates put little or no preparation into this area of the selection process. There are so many resources out there available to help you prepare for the tests, there really is no excuse. As I stated earlier, preparation is key to your success.

Start preparing for the assessment centre stage of the selection process straight away. Even before you have completed the application form, start working through the sample test questions in this guide. Just by practising for 15 minutes a day, you will soon start to see progress in your testing abilities.

Only you will know the areas that you are weak in, and you will need to carry out some form of 'self-analysis' to see where you believe you need to improve. Work on your weak areas!

Action points

- Work on the sample test question provided within this guide.
- Consider purchasing more testing booklets. You can obtain these through **www.how2become.com.**

CHAPTER 3

The Civil Enforcement Officer Person Specification and Job Description

THE CIVIL ENFORCEMENT OFFICER PERSON SPECIFICATION AND JOB DESCRIPTION

This short chapter of the guide is, in my opinion, one of the most important ones to take on-board during your preparation, if you are to have any chance of passing the selection process. One of the first things you need to do before you submit your application for the role is to obtain the person specification and job description. These two important documents will tell you what the assessors are looking for from candidates during each stage of the selection process. If you know what they are looking for, then you have far greater chance of succeeding. I can also safely say that it is possible to predict the interview questions from the information contained within these two documents.

To begin with, take a look at the following example person specification for the role of Civil Enforcement Officer:

PERSON SPECIFICATION

Job title and post number: Civil Enforcement Officer

Grade: Grade 4
                                      £17,802 - £19,621

Team: Parking Services Team

Category	Requirements	Essential (E)/ Desirable (D)	Method of Assessment (Application Form/Interview/ Psychometric Testing)
Education/ Training	Valid Driving Licence	E	Application form/interview
	Good basic standard of education	E	Application form/interview
	Must agree to attend relevant training courses for Civil Enforcement Officer standards of expertise (NVQ's etc)	E	Application form/interview
Experience	Evidence of practical experience in one or more areas of activity numbers 1-14 in the job description	E	Application form/interview
Skills and Knowledge	An understanding of current issues in local government	D	Interview
	Accuracy and attention to detail particularly when working to tight deadlines	E	Application form/interview
	Ability to work on own initiative as well as part of a team	E	Application form/interview
	Capacity for innovation	D	Interview
	Ability to show empathy with the public and their perceptions	D	Interview
EDDC competencies	Communicates honestly, openly and clearly	E	Interview/work based role play if applicable
	Accepts responsibility for their own work activities, behaviour and personal development	E	Interview
	Makes every effort to meet the needs and to exceed the expectations of customers	E	Interview
	Demonstrates good working relationships with others, both inside and outside of their usual work team		
	Takes responsibility for getting things done	E	Interview

	Must be able to carry out the tasks as detailed in the job description	E	Interview
	Presentable appearance	E	Interview
	Able to use initiative	E	Interview
Other relevant factors	Prepared to work weekends, bank holidays and shift patterns	E	Interview
	Committed to equal opportunities	E	Interview
	Ability to work in a nonsmoking environment	E	Interview
	Must be prepared to under-go Disclosure of Criminal Records procedures	E	Interview

You will note on the form that there are both ESSENTIAL and DESIRABLE criteria. It is your job to make sure you absolutely meet the ESSENTIAL criteria and try your hardest to match as many DESIRABLE criteria as possible. The more DESIRABLES you meet, the greater chance of success you will have. You will also note that, in the right hand column, you are made aware of the method of assessment for each particular area. This means you have the knowledge to predict when you will be required to provide details and evidence of where you meet each ESSENTIAL and DESIRABLE criteria. Based on this information, the following DESIRABLES and ESSENTIALS are going to be assessed at interview:

- An understanding of current issues in local government;
- Accuracy and attention to detail particularly when working to tight deadlines;
- Ability to work on own initiative as well as part of a team;
- Capacity for innovation;
- Ability to show empathy with the public and their perceptions.

The way to demonstrate that you meet each of these DESIRABLES is to prepare yourself for the following interview questions:

Q1. What can you tell us about the current issues in local government with regards to civil enforcement?

TIP: prior to your interview read the local newspapers and also visit the Local Authorities website to find out what issues are current. Another great piece of advice is to contact your local MP and arrange a meeting with him or her. During the meeting you can ask them for their advice on what the local issues are.

Q2. Can you give an example of when you have carried out a task using accuracy and attention to detail, particularly when working to tight deadlines?

TIP: Before you attend the interview make sure you have a specific response to this question. You need to ensure that you can give a good response to this question of where you have previously worked to a tight deadline whilst using accuracy and attention to detail.

Q3. Can you give an example of when you have worked on your own initiative and also as well as part of a team?

TIP: Once again, prior to interview make sure you can provide a specific example in response to this question. Check out the interview section of this guide for sample responses and tips to assist you.

Q4. Can you give an example of when you have used your own initiative whilst in a work-related situation?

Q5. How would you demonstrate empathy to members of the public whilst working as a Civil Enforcement Officer?

Q6. Can you give an example of when you have communicated both honestly, openly and clearly?

Q7. How do you currently take responsibility for your own work activities, behaviour and personal development?

Q8. Can you give an example of when you have delivered excellent customer service?

Q9. How do you take responsibility for getting things done?

Q10. Are you prepared to work weekends, bank holidays and shift patterns? Can you give examples of when you have previously worked in these types of situation?

Hopefully you are now beginning to learn how to match the assessable areas during each stage of the selection process. As you can see from the above tutorial, it is certainly possible to predict the interview questions from the person specification! Now let's take a look at a sample job description and how we can use this to further prepare ourselves for selection.

JOB DESCRIPTION

Post title and number	**Civil Enforcement Officers**
Team	**Parking Services**
Responsible to	**Assistant Parking Services Manager**
Responsible for	**No supervisory responsibility**

Job purpose

To carry out patrols of designated areas, both in the Council's off-street car parks and on-street, to ensure compliance with the Council's statutory duties relating to Parking Places Orders in Council Car Parks and on- street Traffic Orders.

To ensure that all Council controlled pay and display machines are in working order. Issue Penalty Charge Notices in respect of vehicles parking in contravention of Parking Places Orders and/or Traffic Orders. Provide information and assistance to the general public.

Key activities

1. Carrying out designated patrols of car parks and streets that come within the Council's jurisdiction.

2. Checking pay and display machines in car parks and on-street in accordance with the manufacturer's instructions.

3. If a machine is not functioning properly, remedy the malfunction or report the fault to the maintenance contractor and Senior Car Park Inspector immediately.

4. Re-stocking pay and display machines with tickets. Collect cash where necessary (this duty will normally be the responsibility of contractors employed for this specific purpose).

5. Identifying that vehicles parked in the car parks are parked in compliance with the Parking Places Orders and that vehicles parked on-street are in compliance with the Traffic Orders.

6. Issuing Penalty Charge Notices in respect of vehicles not parking in compliance with Parking Places Orders and/or Traffic Orders.

7. Assisting in the good order of car parks e.g. maintain reserved spaces for coaches, etc., report on defective, damaged or misleading signs, or other matters requiring attention from Council departments and which may invalidate the issue of a Penalty Charge Notice.

8. Inspect and report immediately any defective or incorrect signs or surface markings located on-street that may invalidate the issue of a Penalty Charge Notice.

9. Assisting where necessary in carrying out surveys of the use made of car parking facilities.

10. The operation and use of necessary plant and equipment including radios, mobile phones, handhelds, printers, cameras etc.

11. Assisting with the implementation of enforcement procedures including clerical duties and attendance at Court.

12. Providing information and assistance to the general public.

13. Noting and reporting on any matter requiring attention of Council departments.

14. Carry out beach equipment inspections and other enforcement inspections where and when applicable.

15. Support your team in ensuring that our services and policies identify, address, and promote the needs of all of our diverse community. This includes the need for safety of children and other vulnerable people.

16. Perform any other relevant activities, commensurate with the grading of the post, in negotiation with the Manager.

You will note that, within the person specification, it states the following as one of the ESSENTIAL criteria:

Evidence of practical experience in one or more areas of activity numbers 1-14 in the job description (assessed at application form stage and interview)

It is your task to work through the key activities indicated on the job description and attempt to match as many as possible. Although you are only required to meet one out of the fourteen, you should try to match as many as possible. Remember, it is asking you to provide evidence of 'practical experience' in one of more of the key areas. Of course, you cannot actually carry out the specific key activities yet because you are not a Civil Enforcement Officer; however, you can provide evidence of practical capabilities in similar related activities. Here are a few examples to help you:

Re-stocking pay and display machines with tickets. Collect cash where necessary (this duty will normally be the responsibility of contractors employed for this specific purpose).

For this particular key activity you may have had to carry out a replenishing of stock task whilst at work in your current job or perhaps you have helped to 'cash-up' at the end of a working day?

Inspect and report immediately and defective or incorrect signs or surface markings located on-street that may invalidate the issue of a Penalty Charge Notice.

To provide practical evidence of this particular task you may have been required to inspect equipment whilst at work and report any defects that you notice.

Support your team in ensuring that our services and policies identify, address, and promote the needs of all of our diverse community. This includes the need for safety of children and other vulnerable people.

To provide evidence in this key activity you can offer evidence of practical experience where you have worked with and supported a team activity in a work-related setting.

As you can see, it is entirely possible to really prepare yourself fully for each stage of the selection process using the explanations I have provided within this section. My advice is to obtain a copy of the person specification and the job description for the role you are applying for and work hard to make sure you match all of the assessable areas.

Now let's move on to the application form stage of the guide.

CHAPTER 4

The Application Form

THE APPLICATION FORM

The application form is an important part of the recruitment process. The information you provide on the application form enables the Local Authority to decide whether or not you are short listed for interview and is also used as the basis for the interview itself.

Before you start to complete the application form, read the job description/role profile, candidate specification, which details the essential/desirable qualities of the post holder. Ensure that you fully complete the application, covering all the requirements detailed on the candidate specification. Do not assume that the interviewing panel have knowledge of your experience and skills; tell them about them as they are unable to guess or make assumptions. If you need any assistance in completing the application form due to a disability, then make sure you let the Authority know and they will be more than happy to help you.

Completing the Application Form

The following guidance will assist you in completing your application form. I want to stress from the outset that the majority of Local Authorities will now require you to complete an online application and therefore, the information I have provided which follows is aimed specifically at online applications only.

Job Title and Details

The post title and reference number will be in the advert for the position and will usually be available to select in the online application form. However, if they are not available make sure you find out the reference number as you will need this when completing the application.

Screening Questions

These are questions designed to highlight key requirements of your prospective employment at the Local Authority and the role itself.

For example, all employees are required to have permission to work in the UK, either through nationality or the Border Agency. Some roles will require specific experience and/or qualifications and you may be asked about these in this section.

Education, Qualifications and Training

Primary school details are not required, but you will be required to give details of your education and qualifications obtained throughout your education. This includes any qualifications which you are studying at the time of your application. Details of recent/relevant training courses should also be given and if you have obtained a level 2 award for Civil Enforcement Officers or other similar award then you should state this within this section.

If you have gained qualifications overseas which you feel are relevant, be sure to provide details in this section. The assessors with then check (if they need to) whether or not they are valid.

If you are invited for interview you will be asked to produce proof of any relevant qualification(s) e.g. your certificate(s).

Present/Most Recent Employment/ Previous Employment or Voluntary Work

This section tells the assessors about your previous employment record, providing a brief description of the duties and responsibilities of the job. Make sure you include all jobs whether full time/ temporary/ part time/ voluntary or any periods of self-employment. This will also be a great place to add any charity or unpaid work you have carried out here. Employment dates should be continuous and if you have had any gaps in employment, you need to tell them why; i.e. a career break, a period of studying, caring for children or parents, unemployment, etc.

Competency Based Questions

These questions are based on the candidate specification and are designed to focus your knowledge, skills and experience on key aspects of the role. There is sometimes also an open section for you to provide the application form assessors with clear examples on how your skills, knowledge or experience meet the needs of the job. The candidate specification will give you an insight into what they are looking for.

Employment References

You must give details of a referee who can give the Local Authority an assessment of your suitability for the post of Civil Enforcement Officer. Personal references are not acceptable. Also, check in advance with your referee that they are happy to be contacted for a reference. If you are currently employed, your referee must be your current employer. If currently unemployed, your referee should be your most recent employer. Otherwise, it could be your job adviser, head teacher/ course tutor if you are still at school.

Health Screening

If selected, you will be required to undergo a health screening process which is appropriate to the post for which you have applied. This normally involves you completing a confidential health questionnaire form, which is then forwarded to the Occupational Health Service for an assessment of your fitness for the post. If Occupational Health require further information from you such as information from your GP, or if they wish to see you they will contact you directly.

Disclosing Criminal Convictions

Certain criminal convictions are 'spent' (forgotten) after a rehabilitation period and you are unlikely to need to inform the Local Authority about these during your application. I would encourage you to confirm this information by visiting the Local Authority website you are applying to join.

However, there are a number of posts within the Local Authority which are exempt from the Rehabilitation of Offenders Act 1974. These posts normally involve working with children or vulnerable adults (e.g. play staff and Sheltered Housing staff) and also some posts in finance and the law. If the post for which you are applying is an exempt post you must declare all convictions - spent and unspent - and any cautions or bind overs.

On the following pages I have provided you with a sample paper-based application form to give you a better understanding of what it might look like and the questions asked. Following the sample application form, I will provide you with a number of sample competency-based questions and answers to assist you when completing your form.

APPLICATION FOR EMPLOYMENT

Please complete the form in block capitals using black ink. Make sure you fill out this form providing ALL the information required. Remember to sign the application before returning it.

VACANCY APPLIED FOR: _____ **LOCATION:** _____

Section A – Personal Details

Surname: _____ Title: Dr/Mr/Mrs/Ms/Miss/Other: _____

Forename(s): _____ Previous Name(s): _____

Home Address: _____
_____ Post Code: _____

    Contact Address (if different from home address): _____
_____ Post Code: _____

Home Phone (Landline): _____ Mobile Phone: _____

Email: _____
National Insurance number ☐☐☐☐☐☐☐☐☐

Section B – Miscellaneous

Have you previously been employed by this authority?   YES ☐   NO ☐

If YES - From: _____ to: _____ Location: _____

How did you learn about this position? _____

Do you have any special needs with which you may require assistance either in the position or at interview stage?

YES ☐   NO ☐   If YES please give details _____

If you are currently working, how much notice are you required to give?

_____

Do you have any relatives working for this authority?   **YES/ NO** If yes please give details

Name _____   Location _____

Where did you hear about the job vacancy? _____

Do you have any IT Skills? If so please give details _____

Section C – Education/Training & Qualifications

Name of School/College/ University Attended Since Age 11	Town/City	Date Started	Date Finished

Qualifications and Certificates Obtained: Include for example RSA, City & Guilds, GCSE's, O and A Levels, NVQ's, Degree and Professional Qualifications/Bodies

Subject	Qualification Obtained	Grade/Level/Pass Mark

Section D – Employment History

Please list your previous employment for at least the last 10 years. Start with your present employer and work backwards. Explain any periods of unemployment/gaps in your work history.

From	To	Organisation Details	Job Title and Brief Description of Duties	Reasons for Leaving
		Organisation: Address: Post Code: Telephone: Reporting to:		
		Organisation: Address: Post Code: Telephone: Reporting to:		
		Organisation: Address: Post Code: Telephone: Reporting to:		
		Organisation: Address: Post Code: Telephone: Reporting to:		
		Organisation: Address: Post Code: Telephone: Reporting to:		
		Organisation: Address: Post Code: Telephone: Reporting to:		

Please continue on a separate sheet if necessary

Attendance Record: - Please give details of the number of days' and reasons for absence due to injury or illness in that you have had in the most recent 12 months of employment.

Number of days of absence & reasons._____

Section E – References

Work references will be taken up from the information you have supplied in Section D. In addition you must be able to provide the names of two people who can provide character references for you. Character references from relatives will not be accepted. See guidelines for further details.

Name, Job Title and Address	Relationship to you and how long known	Telephone	E-mail Address
Post Code			
Post Code			

Section F – Personal Qualities/Skills/Knowledge/Experience

Please state the relevant qualities, skills, knowledge and experience that you could bring to the role:

Please continue on a separate sheet if necessary

Section G – Driving Licence

Do you hold a full current UK or European driving licence?	YES	NO
If not, do you hold a provisional/motorbike licence?	YES	NO
Do you have any current endorsements?	YES	NO

If YES give details: _____

How long have you held your full driving licence? _____

Do you have any other licences e.g. HGV, LGV, PSV, PCV _____

Section H – Declarations

Rehabilitation of Offenders Act 1974

Do you have any unspent Criminal convictions? **YES / NO**   If YES please give full details:

Are you currently subject to any pending Civil or Criminal prosecutions?   **YES/NO**
If yes, please give details: _____

_____

N.B. Once employed by this authority an employee must inform the company of any criminal prosecution or convictions. Failure to do so could result in disciplinary action up to and including dismissal.

Right to Work in the UK

Do you have the Right to Work in the UK?   **YES / NO**

Do you currently have a valid work permit?   **YES / NO**

Should you be successful in your application, we will need to see this or other relevant documentation before an offer of employment is confirmed.

Further background
Have you been subject to personal or business related bankruptcies?   **YES/NO**

If YES please give details;- _____

Have you been or are you subject any county court judgments (CCJs) or defaults registered against
you?   **YES/NO**
If YES please give details; - _____

Do you have any involvement in external businesses please list details of any company directorships
held.   **YES/NO**
If YES please give details; - _____

Have you been or are you subject to disciplinary proceedings, suspensions or
expulsions by any regulatory or professional body or association in relation to your
business or professional activities?
                                                             YES/NO
If YES please give details;- _____

Have you ever been involved in an Employment tribunal?   **YES/NO**
If YES, please give details: _____

SAMPLE COMPETENCY-BASED APPLICATION FORM QUESTIONS AND ANSWERS

Please note: the following questions and answers are also perfect preparation for the interview.

SAMPLE QUESTION

Please state the relevant qualities, skills, knowledge and experience that you could bring to the role.

This type of question is designed to assess whether or not you have the skills, qualities, knowledge and experience to perform the role safely and competently. The question is asking specifically for four different areas; therefore, your response should cater for all of them. In order to assist you during your preparation for this question I have provided a sample response.

SAMPLE ANSWER

The qualities and skills I possess include being observant, good communication skills, calm under pressure, team-worker, an ability to work alone and unsupervised, confident, resilient, able to follow rules and guidelines and also professional and safety conscious. I have knowledge of the Local Authorities codes of conduct and equality policy and I have also undertaken a level 2 award for Civil Enforcement Officers. I have experience in all of the assessable areas including an understanding of current issues in local government, accuracy and attention to detail, particularly when working to tight deadlines, a capacity for innovation and I am also able to show empathy with the public and their perceptions.

SAMPLE QUESTION

Please give details of when you have dealt with a difficult situation.

As a Civil Enforcement Officer you will be required to take responsibility for dealing with difficult situations, especially when dealing with irate owners of vehicles! This question is designed to see whether or not you have any experience of taking responsibility for difficult situations and, more importantly, resolving them. Take a look at the following sample response to this question.

SAMPLE ANSWER

One evening I was sat at home watching television when I heard my next door neighbours smoke alarm sounding. This is not an unusual occurrence as she is always setting off the alarm whilst cooking. However, on this occasion, something was different as the alarm did not normally sound so late at night. I got up out of my chair and went to see if she was OK. She is a vulnerable, elderly lady and I always look out for her whenever possible. When I arrived next door I peered through the window and noticed my neighbour sat asleep on the chair in the front room. Wisps of smoke were coming from kitchen so I knew that she was in trouble. I immediately ran back into my house and dialled 999 calmly. I asked for the Fire Service and the Ambulance Service and explained that a person was stuck inside the house with a fire burning in the kitchen. I provided the call operator as much information as possible including landmarks close to our road to make it easier for the Fire Service to find. As soon as I got off the phone I immediately went round the back of my house to climb over the fence. Mrs Watson, my neighbour, usually leaves her back door unlocked until she goes to bed. I climbed over the fence and tried the door handle. Thankfully the door opened. I entered into the kitchen and turned off the gas heat which was burning dried up soup. I then ran to the front room, woke up Mrs Watson and carried her carefully through the front door, as this was the nearest exit. I then sat Mrs Watson down on the pavement outside and placed my coat around her. It wasn't long before the Fire Service arrived and they took over from them on in. I gave them all of the details relating to the incident and informed them of my actions when in the kitchen.

SAMPLE QUESTION

Please give details of when your communications skills made a difference to a situation.

Being able to communicate effectively both in writing and verbally is crucial to the role of a Civil Enforcement Officer. Not only will you have to speak face-to-face with many vehicle owners each day during your shift, but you will also have to communicate with the parking office and other members of the Local Authority team, including wardens and police officer's. Take a look at the following sample response to this question.

SAMPLE ANSWER

My next door neighbour had a cat they had looked after for years and they were very fond of it. I had to inform them that their cat had just been run over by a car in the road. I was fully aware of how much they loved their cat and I could understand that the message I was about to tell them would have been deeply distressing. They had cherished the cat for years and to suddenly lose it would have been a great shock to them. To begin with I knocked at their door and ask calmly if I could come in to speak to them. Before I broke the news to them I made them a cup of tea and sat them down in a quiet room away from any distractions. I then carefully and sensitively told them that their cat had passed away following an accident in the road. At all times I took into account their feelings and I made sure I delivered the message sensitively and in a caring manner. I took into account where and when I was going to deliver the message. It was important to tell them in a quiet room away from any distractions so that they could grieve in peace. I also took into account the tone in which I delivered the message and I also made sure that I was sensitive to their feelings. I also made sure that I would be available to support them after I had broken the news. I strongly believe that the manner in which I communicated and delivered the message was helpful to the already difficult situation.

FINAL TIPS FOR CREATING A SUCCESSFUL APPLICATION FORM

- Read the form carefully before starting to complete it. Also be sure to read all of the accompanying guidance notes, person specification and job description.

- Follow all instructions carefully. Your form can be rejected for failing to follow simple instructions.

- If you are completing a handwritten version of the form make sure your handwriting is neat, legible, concise and grammatically correct. You will lose marks for incorrect spelling!

- Before you submit the form get somebody to check over it for you.

- Once you have completed the form make sure you make a photocopy of it. You may be asked questions that relate to your responses during the interview.

- Send the form recorded delivery if completing a paper-based version. I have known of many application forms to go missing in the post.

CHAPTER 5

Sample test questions

SAMPLE TEST QUESTIONS

Once you have successfully passed the application form stage you will normally required to undertake an assessment which consists of numeracy and literacy tests. Within this section of the guide we have provided you with a number of practice questions. Whilst these questions will not be the same as the ones you will encounter during the actual test, they are great for your preparation, especially if it has been some time since you sat any type of job-related test or assessment.

The time limit for each test is supplied at the start.

SAMPLE TEST NUMBER 1

Within sample test number 1 there are 30 questions and you have 10 minutes to complete it.

Question 1

Which of the following words is the odd one out?

A. Car   **B.** Aeroplane   **C.** Train   **D.** Bicycle   **E.** House

Answer

Question 2

Which of the following is the odd one out?

A. Right   **B.** White   **C.** Dart   **D.** Bright   **E.** Sight

Answer

Question 3

The following sentence has one word missing. Which word makes the best sense of the sentence?

The mechanic worked on the car for 3 hours. At the end of the 3 hours he was _____ .

A. Home   **B.** Rich   **C.** Crying   **D.** Exhausted   **E.** Thinking

Answer

Question 4

The following sentence has 2 words missing. Which two words make best sense of the sentence?

The man _ _ _ _ _ _ _ _ to walk along the beach with his dog. He threw the stick and the dog _ _ _ _ _ _ _ _ it.

A. hated/chose **B.** decided/wanted **C.** liked/chased
D. hurried/chased **E.** hated/loved

Answer

Question 5

In the line below, the word outside of the brackets will only go with three of the words inside the brackets to make longer words. Which ONE word will it NOT go with?

A	**B**	**C**	**D**
In (direct	famous	desirable	cart)

Answer

Question 6

In the line below, the word outside of the brackets will only go with three of the words inside the brackets to make longer words. Which ONE word will it NOT go with?

A	**B**	**C**	**D**
In (decisive	reference	destructible	convenience)

Answer

Question 7

In the line below, the word outside of the brackets will only go with three of the words inside the brackets to make longer words. Which ONE word will it NOT go with?

	A	**B**	**C**	**D**
A	(float	bout	part	peck)

Answer

Question 8

Which of the following words is the odd one out?

A. Pink   **B.** Salt   **C.** Ball   **D.** Red   **E.** Grey

Answer

Question 9

Which of the following words is the odd one out?

A. Run   **B.** Jog   **C.** Walk   **D.** Sit   **E.** Sprint

Answer

Question 10

Which of the following words is the odd one out?

A. Eagle   **B.** Plane   **C.** Squirrel   **D.** Cloud   **E.** Bird

Answer

Question 11

Which of the following words is the odd one out?

A. Gold   **B.** Ivory   **C.** Platinum   **D.** Bronze   **E.** Silver

Answer

Question 12

Which of the following is the odd one out?

A. Pond   **B.** River   **C.** Stream   **D.** Brook   **E.** Ocean

Answer

Question 13

Which of the following is the odd one out?

A. Wood   **B.** Chair   **C.** Table   **D.** Cupboard   **E.** Stool

Answer

Question 14

Which three letter word can be placed in front of the following words to make a new word?

Time   Break   Light   Dreamer

Answer

Question 15

Which four letter word can be placed in front of the following words to make a new word?

Box   Bag   Age   Card

Answer

Question 16

The following sentence has one word missing. Which ONE word makes the best sense of the sentence?

After walking for an hour in search of the pub, David decided it was time to turn _____ and go back home.

A. up   **B.** in   **C.** home   **D.** around   **E.** through

Answer

Question 17

The following sentence has one word missing. Which ONE word makes the best sense of the sentence?

We are continually updating the site and would be _____ to hear any comments you may have.

A. Pleased   **B.** Worried   **C.** Available   **D.** Suited   **E.** Scared

Answer

Question 18

The following sentence has two words missing. Which TWO words make the best sense of the sentence?

The Fleet Air Arm is the Royal Navy's air force. It numbers some 6,200 people, _____ is 11.5% of the _____ Royal Naval strength.

A. which/total   **B.** and/total   **C.** which/predicted
D. and/corporate

E. which/approximately

Answer

Question 19

The following sentence has one word missing. Which ONE word makes the best sense of the sentence?

The Navy has had to _____ and progress to be ever prepared to defend the British waters from rival forces.

A. develop **B.** manoeuvre **C.** change **D.** seek   **E.** watch

Answer

Question 20

Which of the following is the odd one out?

A. Cat   **B.** Dog   **C.** Hamster   **D.** Owl   **E.** Rabbit

Answer

Question 21

Which word best fits the following sentence?

My doctor says I _____ smoke. It's bad for my health.

A. will   **B.** wouldn't   **C.** shouldn't   **D.** like   **E.** might

Answer

Question 22

Which word best fits the following sentence?

The best thing for a hangover is to go to bed and sleep it _____.

A. through   **B.** over   **C.** away   **D.** in   **E.** off

Answer

Question 23

Complete the following sentence:

By the time Jane arrived at the disco, Andrew _____.

A. hadn't gone   **B.** already left   **C.** has already Left
D. had stayed   **E.** had already left

Answer

Question 24

Which of the following words is the odd one out?

A. Lawnmower   **B.** Hose   **C.** Rake   **D.** Carpet   **E.** Shovel

Answer

Question 25

Complete the following sentence:

Karla was offered the job _____ having poor qualifications.

A. although   **B.** even though   **C.** with   **D.** without   **E.** despite

Answer

Question 26

Complete the following sentence:

Not only _____ to Glasgow but he also visited many other places in Scotland too.

A. did she   **B.** did he   **C.** did he go   **D.** she went   **E.** she saw

Answer

Question 27

Complete the following sentence:

Now please remember, you _____ the test until the teacher tells you to.

A. shouldn't   **B.** will not be starting   **C.** are not to   **D.** can't
E. are not to start

Answer

Question 28

Which of the following is the odd one out?

A. Strawberry **B.** Raspberry **C.** Peach **D.** Blackberry
E. Blueberry

Answer

Question 29

Which of the following is the odd one out?

A. Football **B.** Wrestling **C.** Table tennis **D.** Golf **E.** Rugby

Answer

Question 30

Which of the following is the odd one out?

A. Man **B.** Milkman **C.** Secretary **D.** Police Officer **E.** Firefighter

Answer

Now that you have completed sample test number 1, check your
answers carefully before moving on to the next batch of questions

ANSWERS TO SAMPLE TEST NUMBER 1

1. E

2. C

3. D

4. C

5. D

6. B

7. D

8. D

9. D

10. C

11. B

12. A

13. A

14. Day

15. Post

16. D

17. A

18. A

19. A

20. D

21. C

22. E

23. E

24. D

25. E

26. C

27. E

28. C

29. B

30. A

SAMPLE TEST NUMBER 2

In this exercise you have to choose which word is missing in the sentence the options provided. There are 15 questions in the test and you have 5 minutes to complete it.

Question 1

I want to buy a new pair of jeans because I've put on _____ and my waist has expanded.

A. wait

B. weight

C. wheat

D. waite

Answer

Question 2

This week I felt so weak, I don't know why, maybe because I _____ nothing for days.

A. ate

B. eat

C. hate

D. eaten

Answer

Question 3

He'll go back to his country when there is _____ but he might have to wait for years.

A. peice

B. peece

C. peese

D. peace

Answer

Question 4

The new train was stationary for hours because of the _____ .

A. whether

B. weather

C. wether

D. weaver

Answer

Question 5

_____ country is too dangerous so they're allowed to stay here.

A. Their

B. They're

C. There

D. Thare

Answer

Question 6

I _ _ _ _ _ _ _ some meat away because it tasted awful.

A. through
B. thru
C. threw
D. freed

Answer

Question 7

He _ _ _ _ _ _ _ his nose is big and people stare.

A. nose
B. knose
C. knows
D. nows

Answer

Question 8

_ _ _ _ _ _ _ have to wait until tomorrow to get the results.

A. Heal
B. Hell
C. He'll
D. Heel

Answer

Question 9

Please do not worry, you are _____ alone.

A. not

B. knot

C. note

D. knote

Answer [ ]

Question 10

He decided to _____ for a while before carrying on with his journey.

A. paws

B. pores

C. pours

D. pause

Answer [ ]

Question 11

The teacher heaped _____ on the class for their hard work.

A. praise

B. preys

C. prise

D. prays

Answer [ ]

Question 12

Their mother said they were a right _ _ _ _ _ _ _ _ when they got together.

A. pear
B. pair
C. pare
D. paer

Answer

Question 13

The police dog followed the _____.

A. sent
B. cent
C. scent
D. scent

Answer

Question 14

The police decided to _____ the drugs.

A. seas
B. sees
C. seeze
D. seize

Answer

Question 15

Because the other team failed to turn up for the tournament they got through on a _ _ _ _ _ _ _ _ .

A. by

B. buy

C. bye

D. buye

Answer

Now please check your answers carefully before moving onto the next batch of questions.

ANSWERS TO SAMPLE TEST NUMBER 2

1. B

2. A

3. D

4. B

5. A

6. C

7. C

8. C

9. A

10. D

11. A

12. B

13. C

14. D

15. C

SAMPLE TEST NUMBER 3

In this type of test question you will see sentences, each with a missing word. You have a choice of 4 words with which to fill the gap in each sentence. Select the word which best completes each sentence. Give one answer for each question. Study the example before you begin the four exercises to make sure you understand how to do the test.

Sample question 1

Is this the place _____ you saw the accident?

1. which

2. when

3. where

4. who

Answer | where |

Sample question 2

The thief escaped _____ the open gate.

1. under

2. through

3. over

4. on

Answer | through |

Once you understand the sample questions move onto the exercises that follow.

There are 25 questions and you have 12 minutes to complete the test.

Q1. She was told to lock the dog up to stop the danger _ _ _ _ _ _ _ _ again.

1. occuring

2. ocurring

3. occurring

4. ocuring

Answer

Q2. The finder was advised to take the umbrella to the lost _ _ _ _ _ _ _ _ _ _ _ office.

1. propperty

2. proparty

3. property

4. properrty

Answer

Q3. Richard spent literally hours working on the _ _ _ _ _ _ _ _ of work.

1. peace

2. peice

3. pease

4. pees

Answer

Q4. Sarah had to deal with an angry customer, but she did not deal with them _ _ _ _ _ _ _ _ _ _ .

1. properlly

2. properly

3. properley

4. properrly

Answer [   ]

Q5. She was asked to complete the job in the _ _ _ _ _ _ _ _ _ _ manner.

1. usual

2. usule

3. usuall

4. usual

Answer [   ]

Q6. Sarah had no idea _ _ _ _ _ _ _ _ _ _ she was going.

1. were

2. where

3. weir

4. wear

Answer [   ]

Q7. Sarah was the manager of a company and had to _ _ _ _ _ _ _ _ _ _ _ all of the problems.

1. encounter

2. incounter

3. incountar

4. encountar

Answer

Q8. Sarah went to the shops _ _ _ _ _ _ _ _ _ _ she was hungry.

1. because

2. becauz

3. because

4. beecause

Answer

Q9. Charlotte thought the room looked very _ _ _ _ _ _ _ _ _ _ .

1. decodent

2. decadent

3. decodence

4. decadence

Answer

Q10. Sarah thinks she may need to go and see an _ _ _ _ _ _ _ _ _ _ _ .

1. opticion

2. optician

3. opticien

4. optishion

Answer

Q11. The teacher gave the students good _ _ _ _ _ _ _ _ _ _ _ .

1. example

2. exemple

3. examples

4. exemples

Answer

Q12. For a musician you need to have _ _ _ _ _ _ _ _ _ _ _ .

1. creative

2. cretivity

3. creativity

4. creativety

Answer

Q13. In the factory, workers needed to use their _ _ _ _ _ _ _ _ _ _ .

1. initiative

2. initative

3. enitiative

4. initiatives

Answer

Q14. The door to the cabin was left _ _ _ _ _ _ _ _ _ _ .

1. unnlocked

2. unlocked

3. unllocked

4. unloked

Answer

Q15. The argument put forward by Rita had no _ _ _ _ _ _ _ _ _ _ to the case.

1. significanse

2. significans

3. significance

4. significunce

Answer

Q16. The _ _ _ _ _ _ _ _ _ _ were extending the house.

1. builders
2. bilders
3. billders
4. buillders

Answer

Q17. The students were asked to put forward a _ _ _ _ _ _ _ _ _ _ towards the research.

1. propposition
2. proposition
3. proposishun
4. proposishan

Answer

Q18. The glass lens in the _ _ _ _ _ _ _ _ _ _ had smashed.

1. specticles
2. speticuls
3. specticals
4. spectacles

Answer

Q19. On a field trip, the students were asked to _ _ _ _ _ _ _ _ _ _ the natural environment.

1. obsserv

2. observe

3. observation

4. obsurve

Answer [   ]

Q20. The twins wanted to go for a walk but it was _ _ _ _ _ _ _ _ _ _ wet.

1. two

2. too

3. to

4. tooh

Answer [   ]

Q21. The doctors said that the man was in a critical but _ _ _ _ _ _ _ _ _ _ condition.

1. staple

2. stable

3. stayble

4. staball

Answer [   ]

Q22. Sending flowers to a funeral is a _ _ _ _ _ _ _ _ _ _ gesture.

1. foughtful

2. thoughtful

3. faughtful

4. thortfall

Answer

Q23. Geography students are taught how to look after the _ _ _ _ _ _ _ _ _ _ .

1. invironment

2. envirament

3. environment

4. invirenment

Answer

Q24. One of the students in the class always seemed to be a _ _ _ _ _ _ _ _ _ _ .

1. probalem

2. problem

3. problam

4. probelem

Answer

Q25. Steve and Michael _ _ _ _ _ _ _ _ _ _ in a battle of thumb wars.

1. thought

2. fought

3. thwart

4. fault

Answer

Now check your answers before moving on to the next batch of test questions.

ANSWERS TO SAMPLE TEST NUMBER 3

1. occurring

2. property

3. peice

4. properly

5. usual

6. where

7. encounter

8. because

9. decadent

10. optician

11. example

12. creative

13. initiative

14. unlocked

15. significance

16. builders

17. proposition

18. spectacles

19. observe

20. too

21. stable

22. thoughtful

23. environment

24. problem

25. fought

SAMPLE TEST NUMBER 4

Question 1

You should read all of the passage below before you begin the test. You will see that there are missing words in the passage. Fill in each of the 7 blanks by choosing the best word from the list below so that the passage makes sense. You have 5 minutes to complete the question.

However, with the modern games industry thriving on the internet, global connectivity and access to more and more tools and _____ independent or 'indie' developers are _____ through in the industry. Games such as Flappy Bird are being _____ by one person and going on to make $20,000 per day, it's _____ that although the video game industry is becoming _____ competitive it is still open to _____ and anyone who _____ to get a job within it.

7 of the following 12 words have been taken out of the above passage. Choose one word that best fits each blank space. Use your choice of word only once and write it down in the order in which you think it appears in the passage.

proof, greater, knowledge, everyone, distinguished, increasingly, apparent, breaking, wants, created, pampered, responsibility

Question 2

You should read all of the passage below before you begin the test. You will see that there are missing words in the passage. Fill in each of the 9 blanks by choosing the best word from the list below so that the passage makes sense. You have 5 minutes to complete the question.

The _____ of game development studios are made up of the kind of _____ as described above, although there can be _____ specialisation within the art _____ and programming teams _____ a lot of work is _____, particularly in 3D _____, texturing and _____. This opens up the door to become a _____.

9 of the following 12 words have been taken out of the above passage. Choose one word that best fits each blank space. Use your choice of word only once and write it down in the order in which you think it appears in the passage.

structure, specific, design, further, stabilisation, modelling, streamlining, nowadays, freelancer, animation, outsourced, majority

Question 3

You should read all of the passage below before you begin the test. You will see that there are missing words in the passage. Fill in each of the 8 blanks by choosing the best word from the list below so that the passage makes sense. You have 5 minutes to complete the question.

Thirdly comes _____ – The modeller will then look at the _____ provided from the concepts and use that _____ to create _____ models or 2D models (depending on the games _____). The art asset to be created could be the games _____ , vehicles or _____ 3D models are created using software such as Autodesk's Maya or 3D Studio Max. The 3D artist will provide the art that will be used in the final game. However, before it does the work will be passed on for _____ .

8 of the following 12 words have been taken out of the above passage. Choose one word that best fits each blank space. Use your choice of word only once and write it down in the order in which you think it appears in the passage.

> modelling, development, material, art, 3D, apparent, training, character, environment, texturing, design, downsize

Question 4

You should read all of the passage below before you begin the test. You will see that there are missing words in the passage. Fill in each of the 8 blanks by choosing the best word from the list below so that the passage makes sense. You have 5 minutes to complete the question.

> Amidst talks of bringing private _____ firms into _____ , the question simply begs to be asked: does it make _____ to bring private _____ into the police force, when members of staff are _____ but lack the _____ to be able to support officers fully? Would it perhaps make more sense if police _____ were able to rely more on _____ , and would this require PCSOs to have more powers? These are questions that must be asked at a time like this.

8 of the following 12 words have been taken out of the above passage. Choose one word that best fits each blank space. Use your choice of word only once and write it down in the order in which you think it appears in the passage.

> buildings, policing, sense, devolution, available, powers, agencies, PCSO's, forces, security, politicians, craftsmanship

Question 5

You should read all of the passage below before you begin the test. You will see that there are missing words in the passage. Fill in each of the 9 blanks by choosing the best word from the list below so that the passage makes sense. You have 5 minutes to complete the question.

> In recent times, as with most public services, the police force too has _____ unprecedented cuts. _____ of police officers and constables is _____ on the decline due to the severe _____ measures. At the same time, PCSOs whose role is to _____ the police force are _____ with few powers. At a time when the police force needs as much support from its entire staff as possible, should _____ be given more powers that would, arguably, make them more _____ as the keepers of peace and _____ in the community?

9 of the following 14 words have been taken out of the above passage. Choose one word that best fits each blank space. Use your choice of word only once and write it down in the order in which you think it appears in the passage.

> faced, fresh, support, demonstrable, sharply, PCSO's,
> extrapolate, order, equipped, effective, austerity, diversity,
> numbers, beleaguered

Question 6

You should read all of the passage below before you begin the test. You will see that there are missing words in the passage. Fill in each of the 8 blanks by choosing the best word from the list below so that the passage makes sense. You have 5 minutes to complete the question.

All Emergency calls will be _ _ _ _ _ _ _ _ _ _ _ to the Fire position and it is this person that will answer calls initially. Good _ _ _ _ _ _ _ _ _ _ _ skills and _ _ _ _ _ _ _ _ _ _ _ , fast typing onto the Incident Format screen, are _ _ _ _ _ _ _ _ _ _ _ . Once you become _ _ _ _ _ _ _ _ _ _ _ in this you will usually have an appliance _ _ _ _ _ _ _ _ _ _ _ to incident before you finish your call. If the incident is likely to be of a larger nature or on a _ _ _ _ _ _ _ _ _ _ _ for instance, then numerous calls will be received and everyone else, apart from the Radio position, will _ _ _ _ _ _ _ _ _ _ _ calls.

8 of the following 13 words have been taken out of the above passage. Choose one word that best fits each blank space. Use your choice of word only once and write it down in the order in which you think it appears in the passage.

> routed, in-depth, proficient, contagious, accurate,
> misrepresented, essential, motorway, answer, listening,
> en-route, failures, development

Question 7

You should read all of the passage below before you begin the test. You will see that there are missing words in the passage. Fill in each of the 9 blanks by choosing the best word from the list below so that the passage makes sense. You have 5 minutes to complete the question.

If you look at the _ _ _ _ _ _ _ _ _ _ _ cause for those _ _ _ _ _ _ _ _ _ _ chances are you will find that it is confidence related brought about by a feeling of lack of _ _ _ _ _ _ _ _ _ _ _ Someone goes into the assessment centre feeling _ _ _ _ _ _ _ _ _ _ _ than prepared for a portion of the exam perhaps because they have tried to pass one of the tests before and _ _ _ _ _ _ _ _ _ _ _ or perhaps because they know they have not studied enough. This is why _ _ _ _ _ _ _ _ _ _ is essential especially in all matter of ways from _ _ _ _ _ _ _ _ _ _ with another person, practical _ _ _ _ _ _ _ _ _ _ _ with another person, and studying _ _ _ _ _ _ _ _ _ _ _ written assessment questions.

9 of the following 14 words have been taken out of the above passage. Choose one word that best fits each blank space. Use your choice of word only once and write it down in the order in which you think it appears in the passage.

root, disruptive, preparedness, multitude, less, assessment, tie, interviewing, practise, past, shoes, failed, nerves, conglomerate

Question 8

You should read all of the passage below before you begin the test. You will see that there are missing words in the passage. Fill in each of the 8 blanks by choosing the best word from the list below so that the passage makes sense. You have 5 minutes to complete the question.

By _ _ _ _ _ _ _ _ _ _ your time to practise, _ _ _ _ _ _ _ _ _ _ _ and know the assessment _ _ _ _ _ _ _ _ _ _ _ you can walk into the assessment centre with your nerves under _ _ _ _ _ _ _ _ _ _ _ You know you have prepared the best you could, _ _ _ _ _ _ _ _ _ _ _ making costly errors in your preparation, and are ready to take on the assessment tests. Lastly, if necessary, find a place to _ _ _ _ _ _ _ _ _ _ , relax, and remember to be _ _ _ _ _ _ _ _ _ _ and your _ _ _ _ _ _ _ _ _ _ will remain in control.

8 of the following 12 words have been taken out of the above passage. Choose one word that best fits each blank space. Use your choice of word only once and write it down in the order in which you think it appears in the passage.

measured, prioritising, criteria, mitigating, control, meditate, bolster, avoided, prepare, yourself, parliament, nerves, ready, running

Question 9

You should read all of the passage below before you begin the test. You will see that there are missing words in the passage. Fill in each of the 8 blanks by choosing the best word from the list below so that the passage makes sense. You have 5 minutes to complete the question.

The best way to complete this is by _____ an event that has involved you within that _____ . Write it as though the person you are _____ has no idea on the subject, and by reading it would understand the _____ you are explaining. I find that writing in a _____ context helps, as in a step-by-step direction. The more _____ you can put the better, although try not to _____ with useless _____ .

8 of the following 12 words have been taken out of the above passage. Choose one word that best fits each blank space. Use your choice of word only once and write it down in the order in which you think it appears in the passage.

describing, linger, informing, demystify, meeting, process, premeditated, content, information, 'waffle', 'diary', role

Question 10

You should read all of the passage below before you begin the test. You will see that there are missing words in the passage. Fill in each of the 8 blanks by choosing the best word from the list below so that the passage makes sense. You have 5 minutes to complete the question.

What is at the _ _ _ _ _ _ _ _ _ _ _ of this affair is a shocking _ _ _ _ _ _ _ _ _ _ _ of interest. The very same companies that seem to have _ _ _ _ _ _ _ _ _ _ _ their wealthiest clients, mainly _ _ _ _ _ _ _ _ _ _ _ corporations and rich individuals to _ _ _ _ _ _ _ _ _ _ _ tax, are those that have the _ _ _ _ _ _ _ _ _ _ _ to provide expert accountants to _ _ _ _ _ _ _ _ _ _ _ the government on drafting tax laws and regulations. So the firms essentially helped their clients get away without paying tax by _ _ _ _ _ _ _ _ _ _ _ loopholes from the same laws they helped to create.

8 of the following 12 words have been taken out of the above passage. Choose one word that best fits each blank space. Use your choice of word only once and write it down in the order in which you think it appears in the passage.

Heart, heartless, Aided, multiples, advise, power, avoid, distinguished, multinational, conflict, exploiting, rigour

Now check your answers carefully before moving on to the next batch of questions.

ANSWERS TO SAMPLE TEST NUMBER 4

Question 1

However with the modern games industry thriving on the internet, global connectivity and access to more and more tools and knowledge independent or 'indie' developers are breaking through in the industry. Games such as Flappy Bird are being created by one person and going on to make $20,000 per day, it's proof that although the video game industry is becoming increasingly competitive it is still open to everyone and anyone who wants to get a job within it.

- proof
- knowledge
- Everyone
- increasingly
- breaking
- wants
- created

Question 2

The majority of game development studios are made up of the kind of structure as described above although there can be further specialisation within the art, design and programming teams. Nowadays a lot of work is outsourced, particularly in 3D modelling, texturing and animation. This opens up the door to become a freelancer.

- structure
- design
- further
- modelling
- nowadays
- freelancer

- animation
- outsourced
- majority

Question 3

Thirdly comes modelling – The modeller will then look at the art provided from the concepts and use that material to create 3D models or 2D models (depending on the games design). The art asset to be created could be the games character, vehicles or environment. 3D models are created using software such as Autodesk's Maya or 3D Studio Max. The 3D artist will provide the art that will be used in the final game. However, before it does the work will be passed on for texturing.

- modelling
- material
- art
- 3D
- character
- environment
- texturing
- design

Question 4

Amidst talks of bringing private security firms into policing, the question simply begs to be asked: does it make sense to bring private agencies into the police force, when members of staff are available but lack the powers to be able to support officers fully? Would it perhaps make more sense if police forces were able to rely more on PCSOs, and would this require PCSOs to have more powers? These are questions that must be asked at a time like this.

- policing
- sense
- available
- powers
- agencies
- PCSO's
- forces
- security

Question 5

In recent times, as with most public services, the police force too has faced unprecedented cuts. Numbers of police officers and constables is sharply on the decline due to the severe austerity measures. At the same time, PCSOs whose role is to support the police force are equipped with few powers. At a time when the police force needs as much support from its entire staff as possible, should PCSOs be given more powers that would, arguably, make them more effective as the keepers of peace and order in the community?

- faced
- support
- sharply
- pcsos
- order
- equipped
- effective
- austerity
- numbers

Question 6

All Emergency calls will be routed to the Fire position and it is this person that will answer calls initially. Good listening skills and accurate, fast typing onto the Incident Format screen, are essential. Once you become proficient in this you will usually have an appliance en-route to incident before you finish your call. If the incident is likely to be of a larger nature or on a motorway for instance, then numerous calls will be received and everyone else, apart from the Radio position, will answer calls.

- routed
- proficient
- accurate
- essential
- motorway
- answer
- listening
- en-route

Question 7

If you look at the root cause for those nerves chances are you will find that it is confidence related brought about by a feeling of lack of preparedness. Someone goes into the assessment centre feeling less than prepared for a portion of the exam perhaps because they have tried to pass one of the tests before and failed or perhaps because they know they have not studied enough. This is why practise is essential especially in all matter of ways from interviewing with another person, practical assessment with another person, and studying past written assessment questions.

- root
- preparedness
- less
- assessment
- interviewing

- practise
- past
- failed
- nerves

Question 8

By prioritising your time to practise, prepare, and know the assessment criteria you can walk into the assessment centre with your nerves under control. You know you have prepared the best you could, avoided making costly errors in your preparation, and are ready to take on the assessment tests. Lastly, if necessary, find a place to meditate, relax, and remember to be yourself and your nerves will remain in control.

- prioritising
- criteria
- control
- meditate
- avoided
- prepare
- yourself
- nerves

Question 9

The best way to complete this is by describing an event that has involved you within that role. Write it as though the person you are informing has no idea on the subject, and by reading it would understand the process you are explaining. I find that writing in a 'diary' context helps, as in a step-by-step direction. The more content you can put the better, although try not to 'waffle' with useless information.

- Describing
- Informing
- Process
- Content
- information
- 'waffle'
- 'diary'
- Role

Question 10

What is at the heart of this affair is a shocking conflict of interest. The very same companies that seem to have aided their wealthiest clients, mainly multinational corporations and rich individuals to avoid tax, are those that have the power to provide expert accountants to advise the government on drafting tax laws and regulations. So the firms essentially helped their clients get away without paying tax by exploiting loopholes from the same laws they helped to create.

- heart
- aided
- advise
- power
- avoid
- multinational
- conflict
- exploiting

SAMPLE TEST NUMBER 5

On the following pages you will find a number of practice verbal reasoning tests to assist you during your preparation for becoming a Civil Enforcement Officer. Allow yourself 15 minutes to answer the 15 questions. Write your answer down in the box provided.

Read the following information before answering the questions

- Car A is red in colour and has 11 months left on the current MOT. The tax is due in 4 months time. The car has a full service history and has completed 34,000 miles. The car has had 3 owners.

- Car B is black in colour and has a full 12 months MOT. The tax is not due for another 12 months. The car has completed 3,445 miles and has only had 1 owner. There is a full service history with the car.

- Car C is red in colour and has no tax. The MOT is due to run out in 12 weeks time and the car has no service history. The speedometer reading is 134,000 miles and the car has had a total of 11 owners.

- Car D is black in colour and has 11 months left on the current MOT. The tax is due in 6 months time. The car has no service history and has completed 34,000 miles. The car has only had 1 owner.

- Car E is red in colour and has 7 months tax. The MOT runs out in 7 months' time. The car has a partial service history and has completed 97,000 miles. It has had a total of 4 owners.

Question 1

You want a car that is red in colour and has a full service history with less than 100,000 miles. Which car would you choose?

A.	**B.**	**C.**	**D.**	**E.**
Car A	Car B	Car C	Car D	Car E

Answer [　　　　　　　]

Question 2

You want a car that has more than 6 months tax. You are not concerned about the colour but you also want 12 months MOT. Which car would you choose?

A.	**B.**	**C.**	**D.**	**E.**
Car A	Car B	Car C	Car D	Car E

Answer [　　　　　　　]

Question 3

You want a car that is red in colour and has had no more than 4 owners. You want a minimum of 6 months tax. The mileage is irrelevant but you do want at least 7 months MOT. Which car would you choose?

A.	**B.**	**C.**	**D.**	**E.**
Car A	Car B	Car C	Car D	Car E

Answer [　　　　　　　]

Read the following information before answering the questions

- FLIGHT A, outbound, leaves at 8am and arrives at 1pm. The cost of the flight is £69 but this does not include a meal or refreshments. The return flight departs at 3am and arrives at its destination at 8am.

- FLIGHT B, outbound, leaves at 3pm and arrives at 8pm. The cost of the flight is £97 and this includes a meal and refreshments. The return flight departs at 1pm and arrives at its destination at 5pm.

- FLIGHT C, outbound, leaves at 4pm and arrives at 10pm. The cost of the flight is £70 but this does not include a meal or refreshments. The return flight departs at 10am and arrives at its destination at 4pm.

- FLIGHT D, outbound, leaves at midnight and arrives at 3am. The cost of the flight is £105, which does include a meal and refreshments. The return flight departs at 3pm and arrives at 6pm.

- FLIGHT E, outbound, leaves at 5am and arrives at 12noon. The cost of the flight is £39, which includes a meal and refreshments. The return flight departs at 5pm and arrives at its destination at midnight.

Question 1

You want a flight where the outbound flight arrives before 2pm on the day of departure. You don't want to pay any more than £50. Which flight would you choose?

A.	**B.**	**C.**	**D.**	**E.**
Flight A	Flight B	Flight C	Flight D	Flight E

Answer [   ]

Question 2

You don't want to pay more than £100 for the flight. You want a meal and the outbound departure time must be in the afternoon. Which flight would you choose?

A.	**B.**	**C.**	**D.**	**E.**
Flight A	Flight B	Flight C	Flight D	Flight E

Answer

Question 3

You want a return flight that departs in the afternoon between 12noon and 6pm. The cost of the flight must be below £100 and you do want a meal. The return flight must arrive at your destination before 6pm. Which flight would you choose?

A.	**B.**	**C.**	**D.**	**E.**
Flight A	Flight B	Flight C	Flight D	Flight E

Answer

Read the following information before answering the questions

Janet and Steve have been married for 27 years. They have a daughter called Jessica who is 25 years old. They all want to go on holiday together but cannot make up their minds where to go. Janet's first choice would be somewhere hot and sunny abroad. Her second choice would be somewhere in their home country that involves a sporting activity. She does not like hill climbing or walking holidays but her third choice would be a skiing holiday. Steve's first choice would be a walking holiday in the hills somewhere in their home country and his second choice would be a sunny holiday abroad. He does not enjoy skiing. Jessica's first choice would be a skiing holiday and her second choice would be a sunny holiday abroad. Jessica's third choice would be a walking holiday in the hills of their home country.

Question 1

Which holiday are all the family most likely to go on together?

A. Skiing   **B.** Walking   **C.** Holiday Abroad
D. Sporting activity holiday   **E.** Cannot say

Answer [   ]

Question 2

If Steve and Jessica were to go on holiday together where would they be most likely to go?

A. Sunny holiday abroad   **B.** Skiing   **C.** Cannot say
D. Sporting activity holiday   **E.** Walking

Answer [   ]

Question 3

Which holiday are Janet and Steve most likely to go on together?

A. Cannot say   **B.** Walking   **C.** Sporting activity holiday
D. Skiing   **E.** Sunny holiday abroad

Answer [   ]

Read the following information before answering the questions

Barry and Bill work at their local supermarket in the town of Whiteham. Barry works every day except Wednesdays. The supermarket is run by Barry's brother Elliot who is married to Sarah. Sarah and Elliot have 2 children called Marcus and Michelle who are both 7 years old and they live in the road adjacent to the supermarket. Barry lives in a town called Redford, which is 7 miles from Whiteham. Bill's girlfriend Maria works in a factory in her hometown of Brownhaven. The town of Redford is 4 miles from Whiteham and 6 miles from the seaside town of Tenford. Sarah and Elliot take their children on holiday to Tenford twice a year and Barry usually gives them a lift in his car. Barry's mum lives in Tenford and he tries to visit her once a week at 2pm when he is not working.

Question 1

Which town does Elliot live in?

A.	**B.**	**C.**	**D.**	**E.**
Redford	Whiteham	Brownhaven	Tenford	Cannot say

Answer

Question 2

On which day of the week does Barry visit his mother?

A.	**B.**	**C.**	**D.**	**E.**
Cannot say	Monday	Tuesday	Wednesday	Thursday

Answer

Question 3

Bill and Maria live together in Brownhaven.

A.	**B.**	**C.**
True	False	Cannot say

Answer

Read the following information before answering the questions

- FLAT A is located in a town. It is 12 miles from the nearest train station. It has 2 bedrooms and is located on the ground floor. The monthly rental is £450 and the council tax is £50 per month. The lease is for 6 months.

- FLAT B is located in the city centre and is 2 miles from the nearest train station. It is located on the 3rd floor. The monthly rental is £600 and the council tax is £130 per month. The lease is for 6 months and it has 3 bedrooms.

- FLAT C is located in the city centre and is 3 miles from the nearest train station. It is located on the 1st floor and has 1 bedroom. The monthly rental is £550 and the council tax is £100 per month. The lease is for 12 months.

- FLAT D is located in a town. The monthly rental is £395 per month and the council tax is £100 per month. It is located on the ground floor and the lease is for 6 months. It is 18 miles from the nearest train station. The flat has 2 bedrooms.

- FLAT E is located in a village and is 12 miles from the nearest train station. It has 3 bedrooms and is located on the 2nd floor. The monthly rental is £375 and the council tax is £62.

Question 1

You want a flat that is within 10 miles of the nearest train station and is located on the 1st floor or lower. The combined monthly rent/council tax bill must be no greater than £600. Which flat would you choose?

A.	**B.**	**C.**	**D.**	**E.**
FLAT A	FLAT B	FLAT C	FLAT D	NONE OF THE ABOVE

Answer [   ]

Question 2

You want a flat that has at least 2 bedrooms and has a combined monthly rent/council tax bill that does not exceed £450. Which flat would you choose?

| **A.** | **B.** | **C.** | **D.** | **E.** |
| FLAT A | FLAT B | FLAT C | FLAT D | FLAT E |

Answer [   ]

Question 3

You want a flat that has a combined monthly rent/council tax bill that is not in excess of £600, is within 20 miles of the nearest train station and has a lease of at least 6 months. Which flat would you choose?

| **A.** | **B.** | **C.** | **D.** | **E.** |
| FLAT A | FLAT B | FLAT C | FLAT D | FLAT E |

Answer [   ]

Now check your answers carefully before moving onto the next batch of test questions.

ANSWERS TO SAMPLE TEST NUMBER 5

Test 1

1. A

2. B

3. E

Test 2

1. E

2. B

3. B

Test 3

1. C

2. A

3. E

Test 4

1. B

2. D

3. C

Test 5

1. E

2. E

3. D

SAMPLE TEST NUMBER 6

During sample test number 6 I have provided you with a number of numerical reasoning tests. You have 10 minutes in which to answer the 20 questions. Calculators are not permitted. Please circle your chosen answer.

Question 1

Calculate 5.99 + 16.02

A.	B.	C.	D.	E.
19.01	20.01	21.99	22.99	22.01

Question 2

Calculate 3.47 – 1.20

A.	B.	C.	D.	E.
22.7	2.27	1.27	2.67	0.27

Question 3

Calculate 98.26 – 62.89

A.	B.	C.	D.	E.
37.35	35.37	36.35	36.37	37.73

Question 4

Calculate 45.71 – 29.87

A.	B.	C.	D.	E.
14.84	18.88	14.89	15.84	15.85

Question 5

Calculate 564.87 + 321.60

A.	B.	C.	D.	E.
886.45	886.74	886.47	868.47	868.74

Question 6

Calculate 16.0 – 9.9

A.	B.	C.	D.	E.
6.9	6.1	7.1	7.9	5.1

Question 7

Calculate 1109.12 + 0.8

A.	B.	C.	D.	E.
1109.20	1109.92	1109.02	1110.20	1110.92

Question 8

Calculate 4.1 x 3.0

A.	B.	C.	D.	E.
123	9.1	12.41	7.1	12.3

Question 9

Calculate 16.8 x 4

A.	B.	C.	D.	E.
67.2	64.8	64.47.1	67.4	67.8

Question 10

Calculate 2.2 x 2.2

A.	B.	C.	D.	E.
4.4	44.4	2.84	4.84	8.44

Question 11

In the following question what is the value of t?

$$\frac{5(t - 32)}{2} = 5$$

A.	B.	C.	D.	E.
64	128	43	34	39

Question 12

In the following question what is the value of t?

$$\frac{3(t + 35)}{6} = 35$$

A.	B.	C.	D.	E.
35	70	75	77	30

Question 13

In the following question what is the value of t?

$$\frac{9(t \times 16)}{5} = 144$$

A.	B.	C.	D.	E.
6	3	9	15	5

Question 14

In the following question what is the value of t?

$$\frac{4t - 16}{32} = 2$$

A.	B.	C.	D.	E.
5	10	15	20	25

Question 15

Convert 0.7 to a fraction

A.	B.	C.	D.	E.
$\frac{7}{10}$	$\frac{3}{4}$	$\frac{75}{1}$	$\frac{1}{10}$	$\frac{2}{3}$

Question 16

Convert 2.5 to a fraction

A.	B.	C.	D.	E.
$\frac{25}{1}$	$\frac{3}{6}$	$2\frac{1}{2}$	$\frac{1}{25}$	$2\frac{2}{1}$

Question 17

Convert 3.75 to a fraction

A.	B.	C.	D.	E.
$\frac{75}{1}$	$\frac{1}{375}$	$3\frac{1}{75}$	$\frac{75}{3}$	$3\frac{3}{4}$

Question 18

Convert $\frac{3}{10}$ to a decimal

A.	B.	C.	D.	E.
3.0	0.3	3.33	0.03	0.003

Question 19

Convert $\frac{1}{4}$ to a decimal

A.	B.	C.	D.	E.
0.025	2.5	0.25	0.4	4.0

Question 20

Convert $\frac{4}{5}$ to a decimal

A.	B.	C.	D.	E.
0.08	8.0	4.5	5.4	0.8

Now please check your answers carefully before moving onto the next batch of test questions.

ANSWERS TO SAMPLE TEST NUMBER 6

1. E

2. B

3. B

4. D

5. C

6. B

7. B

8. E

9. A

10. D

11. D

12. A

13. E

14. D

15. A

16. C

17. E

18. B

19. C

20. E

SAMPLE TEST NUMBER 7

In sample test number 7 there are 15 questions and you have 30 minutes to complete it.

Look at Table 1 below and then answer the questions that follow.

TABLE 1. The following table lists the type of bonus each member of staff will receive if they reach a specific number of sales per hour they work. The table has not yet been completed. Staff work seven hour shifts. In order to answer the questions you will need to complete the table.

TIME	10 SALES	20 SALES	30 SALES	40 SALES
1st HOUR	£21.00	£41.50	£60.50	£72.00
2nd HOUR	£18.00	£35.00	£52.00	£60.00
3rd HOUR	£15.00	£28.50	£43.50	£50.00
4th HOUR	-	£22.00	£35.00	£42.00
5th HOUR	£9.00	-	£26.50	£36.00
6th HOUR	£6.00	£9.00	-	£32.00
7th HOUR	£3.00	£3.50	£9.50	-

Note: If a worker achieves 160 sales or more during their 7 hour shift they will receive an additional £50 bonus.

Question 1

If the table was complete how much could a worker earn in bonuses if they reached 10 sales every hour of their 7 hour shift?

A.	B.	C.	D.	E.
£81	£84	£91	£85	£294

Question 2

How much would a worker earn in bonuses if they reached 30 sales per hour for the first 3 hours of their shift and 40 sales per hour for the remaining 4 hours of their shift?

A.	B.	C.	D.	E.
£292	£293	£436	£246	£346

Question 3

How much would a worker earn in bonuses if they reached 10 sales during their first and last hour, 20 sales during the 2nd and 6th hours, 30 sales during the 3rd and 5th hours and 40 sales during the 4th hour?

A.	B.	C.	D.	E.
£230	£250	£180	£181	£182

Look at the table below and then answer the questions that follow.

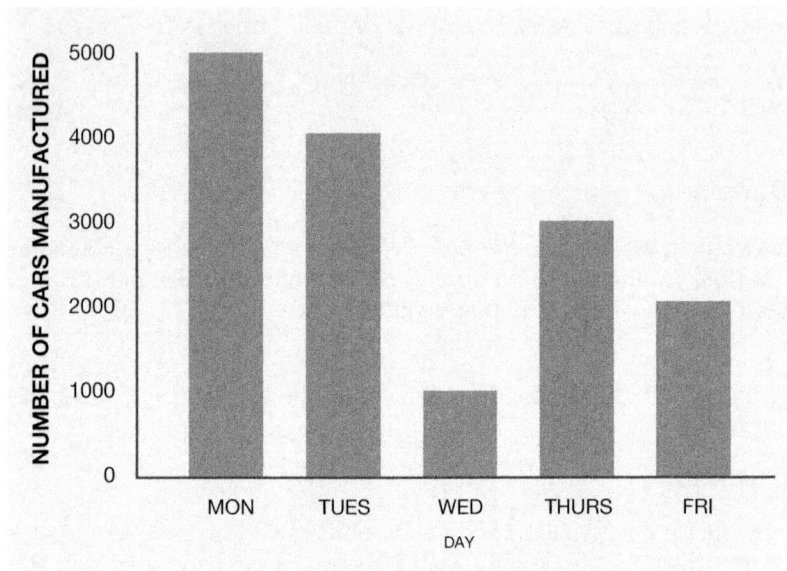

The above chart indicates the total number of cars manufactured per day of the week at the Arlingford Car Depot.

Question 4

On which day was the number of cars manufactured 80% less than the number manufactured on Monday?

A.	B.	C.	D.	E.
Tuesday	Wednesday	Thursday	Friday	None

Question 5

How many cars were produced in total on Tuesday, Wednesday and Friday?

A.	B.	C.	D.	E.
4,000	5,000	6,000	7,000	8,000

Question 6

What was the average number of cars manufactured per day for the working week?

A.	B.	C.	D.	E.
2,142	2,500	3,000	2,141	2,140

The following graph indicates the total monthly profits of four competing companies.

Look at the table below and then answer the questions that follow.

- — ·· — ·· — · **COMPANY A**
- ············· **COMPANY B**
- — — — — — **COMPANY C**
- ▭▭ ▭▭ ▭▭ ▭▭ **COMPANY D**

Question 7

Over the 6 month period, which company made the greatest profit?

A.	**B.**	**C.**	**D.**
Company A	Company B	Company C	Company D

Question 8

What was the difference in profits over the 6 month period between company   C and company D?

A.	**B.**	**C.**	**D.**	**E.**
£1,000	Nothing	£2,000	£3,000	£4,000

Question 9

What was the total combined 6 month profit for all four companies?

A.	**B.**	**C.**	**D.**	**E.**
£66,000	£61,000	£63,000	£65,000	£68,000

The following table shows the distribution list for a UK based company including the location of delivery, type of package ordered, the quantity ordered and the cost excluding delivery.

Look at the table below and then answer the questions that follow.

DATE	LOCATION OF DELIVERY	PACKAGE ORDERED	QUANTITY ORDERED	COST (EXCLUDING DELIVERY)
13th Jan	Kent	Package 1	2	£45
17th Jan	Preston	Package 4	13	£1,600
2nd Feb	Manchester	Package 2	6	£246
3rd Feb	Glasgow		12	£270
17th Feb	Fareham	Package 2	8	
19th Mar	Huddersfield	Package 5	1	£213
20th Mar	Crewe		3	£639

Question 10

Which package will be delivered on the 3rd of February?

A.	B.	C.	D.
Package 1	Package 2	Package 4	Package 5

Question 11

What will be the cost (excluding delivery) on the 17th of February?

A.	B.	C.	D.	E.
£322	£324	£326	£328	£330

Question 12

Which package is scheduled to be delivered to Crewe on the 20th of March?

A.	B.	C.	D.
Package 1	Package 2	Package 4	Package 5

The following bar chart indicates the total number of people employed by a large international distribution company. Study the chart before answering the questions that follow.

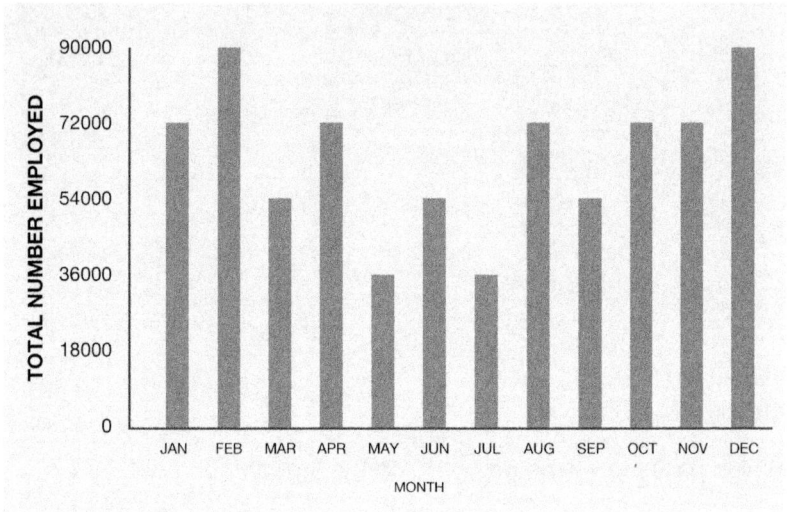

Question 13

What was the average monthly employment figure for the 12 month period?

A.	**B.**	**C.**	**D.**	**E.**
60,000	50,000	54,500	64,500	74,500

Question 14

What was the total number of people employed during the second quarter of the year?

A.	**B.**	**C.**	**D.**	**E.**
62,000	52,000	162,000	152,000	143,000

Question 15

What was the difference between the number of people employed in the first quarter and the last quarter of the year?

A.	B.	C.	D.	E.
18,000	17,000	16,000	180,000	170,000

Now check your answers carefully before moving onto the next test section.

ANSWERS TO SAMPLE TEST NUMBER 7

1. B

2. E

3. C

4. B

5. D

6. C

7. A

8. B

9. E

10. A

11. D

12. D

13. D

14. C

15. A

CHAPTER 6

The listening test

THE LISTENING TEST

As part of the Civil Enforcement Officer test you may be required to sit what is called a listening test. The listening test requires you to listen to a piece of information which is either read out to you by an assessor or pre-recorded on an audio recording device, such as a tape or CD player. Whilst the extract is being read out you are required to listen carefully to the information as you will be required to answer **true, false or cannot say** questions at the end. You are not permitted to take notes during the test.

The type of information that will be read out to you does vary greatly. For example, Kent County Council, at the time of publishing this book, are reading out the Goldilocks story during the listening test. Therefore, the only real way to improve your ability during this test is to actually practice a number of sample test questions.

Within this section of the guide I have provided you with 3 sample tests. In order to make the test as realistic as possible you can either:

1. Ask a friend or relative to read out the extract to you before answering the questions that follow;

2. Download an MP3 of the 5 tests at the following page:

www.CivilEnforcementTests.co.uk

Remember, you are not permitted to take notes whilst the extract is being read out.

LISTENING TEST NUMBER 1 – GOLDILOCKS

The following extract is to be read out to the candidate only once. Once the extract is complete the candidate has 5 minutes to answer the questions that follow.

Once upon a time, there was a little girl named Goldilocks. She lived at the edge of the forest with her family. One morning, while she was picking flowers, Goldilocks wandered into the forest and lost her way. She was very frightened, but then she saw a friendly little cottage in the distance.

The friendly little cottage belonged to three bears. One was a great big Papa Bear, one was a middle-sized Mama Bear, and one was a tiny little Baby Bear. That morning, the three bears decided to take a walk while their porridge – which tastes like oatmeal – was cooling. It was too hot to eat!

Right as they left through the back door, Goldilocks came in through the front door very quietly. The first thing she saw and smelled was the sweet, steamy porridge. "I sure am hungry," Goldilocks said. "I'll just have one bite."

First, she tried a spoonful from Papa Bear's great big bowl. "OW!" she yelled, "TOO HOT!"

Next, she tried a spoonful from Mama Bear's medium-sized bowl. "Brrrrr! TOO COLD!" she complained.

Finally, Goldilocks tried a spoonful from Baby Bear's tiny little bowl. "YUMMY!" she cried. "THIS IS JUST RIGHT!" Goldilocks ate the entire bowlful.

After running around the forest all day, Goldilocks' feet were sore. "I need to sit down for a little while to rest my sore feet!" she thought.

First, she sat in Papa Bear's great big armchair. "TOO HARD!" she screamed. Goldilocks stomped to the next chair.

Next she sat in Mama Bear's medium-sized chair. It was so soft that she sunk in! "TOO SOFT!" she complained, as she pulled herself out of the cushions.

Finally, she sat in Baby Bear's tiny little rocking chair. "JUST RIGHT!" She laughed, and rocked until the chair broke.

With nowhere to sit, Goldilocks climbed up the stairs to find somewhere to sleep. She was still very tired.

First, she tried Papa Bear's great big bed. "TOO HIGH!" she yelled.

Then, she tried Mama Bear's medium-sized bed. "TOO LOW!" she screamed.

Finally, she tried Baby Bear's tiny little bed. "JUST RIGHT!" she sighed. Then Goldilocks fell asleep and dreamed dreams of flowers and warm cookies.

Just then, the three bears returned home from their walk. They saw spoons in their porridge, and were very surprised. "Who's been eating my porridge?" asked Papa Bear.

"Who's been eating my porridge?" asked Mama Bear.

"Who's been eating my porridge and eaten it all up?" cried Baby Bear.

Then, the three bears saw that their chairs had been used. "Who's been sitting in my chair?" Papa Bear howled.

"Who's been sitting in my chair?" wondered Mama Bear.

"Who's been sitting in my chair and BROKEN it?" squeaked Baby Bear.

The three Bears ran upstairs to check their bedrooms. "Who's been sleeping in my bed?" Papa Bear roared.

"Who's been sleeping in my bed?" growled Mama Bear. She was a little angry and a little worried.

"Who's been sleeping in my bed and is STILL HERE?" Baby Bear screamed. He said it so loudly that he woke Goldilocks up.

She was so frightened that she jumped out of bed, ran out the front door, and raced through the forest until she heard her mother's voice. Goldilocks was so happy to see her mother that she promised to never wander through the forest alone again.

QUESTIONS FOR LISTENING TEST 1

You have 5 minutes to answer the following questions.

Q1. The friendly little cottage belonged to Goldilocks.

TRUE
FALSE
CANNOT SAY

Answer [   ]

Q2. Goldilocks fell asleep in Baby Bear's bead.

TRUE
FALSE
CANNOT SAY

Answer [   ]

Q3. Goldilocks fell asleep and dreamed dreams of sweet, steamy porridge.

TRUE
FALSE
CANNOT SAY

Answer [   ]

Q4. **Goldilocks is 10 years old.**

TRUE

FALSE

CANNOT SAY

Answer

Q5. **Goldilocks complained that Mama Bear's medium-sized chair was too hard.**

TRUE

FALSE

CANNOT SAY

Answer

Now check your answers carefully before moving onto the next sample listening test.

ANSWERS TO LISTENING TEST NUMBER 1

Q1. FALSE

Q2. TRUE

Q3. FALSE

Q4. CANNOT SAY

Q5. FALSE

LISTENING TEST NUMBER 2 – THE ROLE OF A CIVIL ENFORCEMENT OFFICER

The following extract is to be read out to the candidate only once. Once the extract is complete the candidate has 5 minutes to answer the questions that follow.

Civil enforcement officers make sure that drivers follow parking regulations on public streets and in car parks. If you enjoy working outdoors and want a responsible role, this job could be a perfect job for you.

You'll need to be assertive and polite when dealing with people. A calm and professional approach will also help you to handle difficult situations. There are no set qualifications to become a Civil Enforcement Officer. Experience of working in a customer service role is highly valued and could help you get into this job.

As a Civil Enforcement Officer you would be patrolling the public streets and local council car parks. Your duties would include:

- patrolling to make sure that regulations are being followed

- recording and issuing Penalty Charge Notices

- checking parking meters and car park equipment, and reporting damage or faults

- checking that car parks are clean and tidy

- reporting defective signs and road markings

- identifying and reporting abandoned vehicles

- explaining regulations to motorists and advising them about parking facilities

- checking tickets and taking payments in some car parks

- working with other professionals like police community support officers or the police to report incidents like crimes or anti-social behaviour

- attending court or tribunal if a parking ticket is being disputed.

You would use equipment such as hand-held computers and printers for recording and issuing Penalty Charge Notices, two-way radios, or mobile phones, to keep in contact with supervisors and also cameras to record vehicles that are breaking parking regulations.

You would usually work shifts between 8am and 8pm but this does vary greatly from authority to authority. This would be on a rota including Saturdays and sometimes Sundays. Some jobs may even be part-time.

You would spend most of the day patrolling on foot and be out in all weathers. You would be expected to wear a uniform and waterproof clothing.

You may use a vehicle to travel between different areas, using a car, motorcycle or moped, depending on your job role.

QUESTIONS FOR LISTENING TEST 2

You have 5 minutes to answer the following questions.

Q1. Duties of a Civil Enforcement Officer include returning abandoned vehicles to their owner.

TRUE

FALSE

CANNOT SAY

Answer

Q2. Civil Enforcement Officers always work from 8am to 8pm.

TRUE

FALSE

CANNOT SAY

Answer

Q3. You will need 3 GCSE's to become a Civil Enforcement Officer.

TRUE

FALSE

CANNOT SAY

Answer

Q4. As a Civil Enforcement Officer you would use equipment such as hand-held computers and printers for recording and issuing Penalty Charge Notices.

TRUE

FALSE

CANNOT SAY

Answer

Q5. The duties of a Civil Enforcement Officer include checking that car parks are clean and tidy.

TRUE

FALSE

CANNOT SAY

Answer

Now check your answers carefully before moving onto the next sample listening test.

ANSWERS TO LISTENING TEST NUMBER 2

Q1. FALSE

Q2. FALSE

Q3. FALSE

Q4. TRUE

Q5. TRUE

LISTENING TEST NUMBER 3 – DEFUSING CONFLICT

Defusing conflict requires at least one person taking action to prevent conflict escalating or to de-escalate situations which have already become destructive, confrontational or aggressive. The approach to defusing conflict involves a process of understanding situations, self-reflection, considering response options, building trust and communicating to influence the outcome of the situation. Each aspect of the approach will now be explained:

Don't do or say what comes spontaneously

Spontaneous responses are often driven by anger or fear which can escalate a conflict situation. Consciously control your immediate reactions by managing your emotions.

Adopt a pro-defusing mind-set

Assume some responsibility for the situation and ensure that it doesn't escalate – no matter what others do. Be non-judgemental, don't make it personal, be prepared to listen and make sure that communication is effective.

Understand the Conflict

How dangerous is the situation? Is it rational? How anxious are those involved? How many conflicts are active and which is most important? Is the conflict about mutually incompatible goals or driven by emotions?

Choose the outcome and response

Identify the outcome you want from the situation and check that it is necessary and achievable in the time available. Then, identify a response to give you the best chance of safely achieving the outcome.

Keep safe – if you are at risk then get away

Personal safety is paramount. Take steps to reduce the risks. Even calm situations can escalate quickly. If your chosen response seems too risky then do something else. If at any point you feel at risk of imminent harm then get away.

Open dialogue

Opening dialogue aims to reduce anger and anxiety; start to build trust; and establish the best chance of achieving the outcome you want. Opening lines are critical; the wrong one could escalate a situation, the right one could defuse a volatile situation altogether.

Continue dialogue

Continue dialogue when defusing a situation requires you to: understand another person's perspective; be understood yourself; or influence another person's behaviour. The aim is to agree a shared understanding of the situation and build trust.

Influence and persuade

Once trust has been established and a shared understanding of the situation agreed it may be possible to facilitate others to modify their attitude, goals or behaviours.

QUESTIONS FOR LISTENING TEST 3

You have 5 minutes to answer the following questions.

Q1. **Part of the defusing conflict process requires you to do or say what comes spontaneously.**

TRUE

FALSE

CANNOT SAY

Answer

Q2. If at any point during the conflict you feel at risk of imminent harm then you must get away.

TRUE

FALSE

CANNOT SAY

Answer

Q3. Conflict is bad for everyone involved.

TRUE

FALSE

CANNOT SAY

Answer

Q4. Opening lines are critical; the wrong one could escalate a situation.

TRUE

FALSE

CANNOT SAY

Answer

Q5. **If your chosen response seems too risky then it is best to give up and walk away.**

TRUE

FALSE

CANNOT SAY

Answer

Now check your answers carefully before moving onto the next sample listening test.

ANSWERS TO LISTENING TEST NUMBER 3

Q1. FALSE

Q2. TRUE

Q3. CANNOT SAY

Q4. TRUE

Q5. FALSE

CHAPTER 7

The Civil Enforcement Officer interview

THE CIVIL ENFORCEMENT OFFICER INTERVIEW

Before I come onto the all-important interview questions and answers I want to first of all write about interview preparation. How you come across during the interview is just as important as responding to the questions. To make it easier to follow, I will break it down into a number of different elements:

Personal appearance

This carries far more weight than people think. First impressions are so important. It says a lot about who you are. Remember that you only get one opportunity to create a first impression. Unless it is specifically not required you should always dress in proper business attire such as a suit and tie or equivalent if you are female.

Your shoes must be clean too, and if you need a haircut, then get it done a few days before. I always advise people to prepare the night before the interview and lay everything out pressed and ready for the morning. Even down to your underwear, which sounds ridiculous, but it is all about limiting the stress that you will already be under on the day of your interview. The last thing you want to be doing is rushing around for your clothes or shoes on the big day only to find you threw away those smart shoes months ago. Be organised in your preparation!

Finally, with regards to personal appearance, you are applying to become a Civil Enforcement Officer, which is a uniformed role – if you cannot present yourself in a smart and presentable manner during the interview, you are hardly going to wear your uniform with pride, are you?

Travelling to the interview

- How are you going to get to the interview?
- Do you know where you are going to park?

- Are the trains or buses running on time?

- Do you need a congestion charge ticket if the interview is in London?

These are all obvious questions but important nonetheless. Again, it is all down to preparation. Remember to take a contact number with you just in case you are going to be late for the interview. Then you can call them well in advance to tell them you will be late due to a breakdown or traffic congestion. If you are travelling by car, don't wear your jacket. Hang it up on a coat hanger so that it is not creased when you arrive for the interview.

Punctuality

This can be related to the above subject but is still just as important. Make sure you leave with plenty of time to spare before your interview. It's far better to arrive an hour early than 5 minutes late! I usually arrive 30 minutes before my interview and sit in the car and re-read the job description for the role or information about the company that I am applying to join.

The interview format

Just by virtue of the fact you have been offered an interview indicates that the employer believes you have the potential to work for them in the role of Civil Enforcement Officer. They will have already carried out a screening process based around the qualities and attributes relating to the post that you have applied for. The interview is designed so that the employer can see you in person and look at your demeanour, presence, personality and appearance along with the opportunity to ask you questions based around your application form and the role that you are applying for.

You may be competing against up to 30 applicants, so it is important that you stand out in a positive way and not for the wrong reasons. The basics of interview etiquette are key to your success, and you need to prepare for these as much as you do the interview questions themselves.

Most interviews will follow the following format:

Introduction and icebreaker

The interviewer should give you a brief overview of the interview and possibly the role that you are applying for. Dependant on the interviewer, you will be given the opportunity to tell the panel about yourself. Your response should be prepared beforehand and you can use this as an opportunity to sell yourself. You should cover brief topics relating to your experience, qualifications, outside interests and ambitions. If you tell the panel that in your spare time you are working towards a qualification that can relate to the role of Civil Enforcement Officer, then this can only be a good thing. Try to keep your introduction as brief as possible and don't go over two minutes in length.

The interview itself

This is the area in which you are asked a series of questions relating to your application form and the post that you have applied for. This is where you should do most of the talking and if you have prepared well enough you will be able to answer most questions, although it is not unusual to find yourself struggling to answer one or two. In this situation it is always best not to waffle. If you really don't know the answer to a particular question then just say so.

The opportunity to ask questions

This is a time for you to ask some questions to the panel. You should usually have two or three questions that you want to ask at the end. I have seen a few people fail interviews at this final stage. I can remember one particular person applying for a role as a firefighter. I was interviewing him for the role and he had answered all of the questions near perfectly. At the end of the interview I asked him whether he had any questions to ask the panel. Here's what he said:

"Yes I do have one question. How have I done? I personally think that I've had a fantastic interview and would I be very surprised if I've failed. Can I have feedback now please?"

The above question should never have been asked. It displayed arrogance and it also put the interview panel in an uneasy situation.

Make sure your questions are relevant but always avoid asking questions relating to leave or salary (unless you are specifically asked). Ask questions that relate to the role of a Civil Enforcement Officer and the development opportunities within the organisation. You may have researched the organisation and found that a new project is being developed within the Parking Services department. Ask them how the project is developing and what plans they have for the future. Don't ask questions where you are trying to be clever or questions that are too technical. If you try to catch them out they won't be impressed and they may come back and ask you a similarly difficult question.

Questions to ask

- If I am successful, how long will it be before I start training? (This shows enthusiasm and motivation.)

- During my research I noticed that you have just implemented a new set of parking restrictions in the area. Has it been successful in reducing congestion within the town? (This shows a caring attitude towards the organisation, and also that you've carried out your research.)

- Even though I don't know yet whether I have been successful at interview, are there any books or literature I could read to find out more about the Parking Services team or the role I have applied for? (This shows commitment.)

Questions to avoid

- How have I done during the interview? Have I passed? (This question demonstrates impatience and a slight level of arrogance. The interview panel will need to time to discuss your performance before making their decision.)

- How much leave will I get in this role? (I don't need to explain why this is a bad question!)

- How quickly can I progress through the company in terms of promotion? (This question, whilst demonstrating a level of enthusiasm, shows the panel that you have little intention of staying in the role long.)

- I have a holiday booked in four weeks' time. If I am successful, can I have the time off? (You haven't even started and you are asking for time off. Wait until you have started in the role before discussing your leave requirements.)

The end of the interview

Make sure you remain positive at this stage and thank the entire panel for their time. This is a good opportunity to shake their hands. If you do shake their hand then make sure it's a firm grip and look them in the eye. There's nothing worse than shaking a person's hand when it feels like a wet lettuce!

At the end of every interview I always leave the panel with a final statement. Here's an example:

"I just want to say thank you for inviting me along to interview. I've really enjoyed the experience and I have learnt a tremendous amount about your company. If I am successful then I promise you that I will work very hard in the role and I will do all that I can to surpass your expectations."

This statement is very powerful. This is the final thing the interview panel will remember you for. When you leave the interview room they are probably going to asses/discuss your performance. Just as first impressions last, so do final impressions also.

Responding to the interview questions

During the interview you will likely be asked two different types of questions; motivational and situational. Motivational questions are in regards to your motivation for applying for the job, such as what preparation you have done before applying and also what you do during your spare time etc. Situational interview questions seek to assess what experience you already have that you can bring to the role, such as examples of when you have worked on your own initiative or when you have had to be flexible in a work-related situation.

When responding to situational interview questions I strongly recommend that you use the S.T.A.R method for constructing your responses. Here's an explanation of what it means:

When constructing your responses to the situational questions within this guide, create them using the following format:

S – situation

Start off by explaining what the situation was and who was involved.

T – task

Now move on and tell the panel what the task was that you were required to carry out or complete.

A – action

Then tell the interview panel what action you took and also what action other people took when trying to complete the task.

R – result

Finish off by telling the panel what the result was following your actions and the actions of the other people involved in the situation. Always try to ensure that the result is a positive one!

If you follow the above method for creating your responses to situational interview questions then your responses will be formulaic, concise and in a logical sequence. This will help you to gain higher scores in the assessable area of effective communication. Let's now move onto a number of sample interview questions and answers to help you prepare. Following each question and sample answer I have provided you with a blank template so that you can create your own response to the question.

Warm-up questions

These types of questions are usually asked at the beginning of an interview. They are sometimes used by an interview panel to give you the opportunity to warm up in preparation for the assessable questions.

Q. How was your journey here today?

This question is very easy to answer. However, avoid single word or short replies such as:

"Yes it was good thanks."

Try to add more substance to your response and use it as an opportunity to talk to the panel and also show them that you have some great qualities such as organisation and preparation.

"Yes it was a good journey thanks. I've never been to this building before so I carried out a dummy run last night. The last thing I wanted was to be late for the interview so I made sure that I prepared fully. I got up early this morning, checked the travel news and then set off with plenty of time to spare. I arrived here 30 minutes early so I sat in my car, composed myself and re-read my notes about the job and your company."

Q. Why have you decided to apply for this job?

This again is a very common interview question and one that needs to be answered carefully. Remember that an interview panel will have heard all of the usual responses such as "I've wanted to work in this kind of role since I was a child", and "This job just really appeals to me". These types of standard responses will gain you few marks.

It is crucial that you provide a response to this type of question that is unique, truthful and different to all of the other candidates.

Consider the following points:

- Provide a response that demonstrates you've carried out plenty of research. During your research something has caught your eye about the job that is very appealing, such as making a difference to the community by ensuring the roads are kept safe and free from congestion. This will demonstrate to the panel that you have looked into the role.

- Consider providing a response that demonstrates you have the key skills required to perform the job competently. An example would be:

"I understand that this role requires an ability to communicate professionally with the general public, an ability to defuse confrontational situations, flexibility and also team working skills. I believe I am very strong in these areas, and therefore I would be a valuable asset to the Parking Services team. Having researched the job and organisation extensively I have noticed a common theme appearing time and time again – professionalism and dedication. I have also spoken to people who already work within the Parking Services team, and the feedback I have received has been excellent. I really want to work for this team and the skills and experience I have already gained will allow me to contribute towards the organisation's goals in a positive manner."

Warm-up questions can come in any format. The main aim for you is to make sure that you speak and communicate with the panel. Always avoid single word answers or short responses. The easy questions are your opportunity to get warmed up, and they are also your chance to create a rapport with the interviewers.

We will now take a look at a number of main interview questions.

Question 1 – Tell me about you?

This is a common introductory question that many interviewers use to break the ice. It is designed to get you talking about something you know – You!

A big mistake usually made by the majority of people is that they focus on their family, children, hobbies or home life. Whilst you may have some interesting facts about your personal life you should either avoid these, unless specifically asked, or keep them very brief. Try to answer this type of question based around your own personal achievements, educational background and ongoing studies. It is good to say that you are motivated or enthusiastic but you MUST ensure that you provide examples or scenarios where this has been proven. For example you might say, "I am a motivated person – whilst working for my previous employer I achieved 'XYZ', which enabled the company to achieve its goal in relation to increased profit margins etc."

Giving specific, brief examples is positive. Remember that anyone can tell an interview panel that they are 'motivated', 'enthusiastic' or 'determined' but not everybody can prove it. Try to think about and use some of the following key words when structuring some of your answers:

- Motivated
- Self-starter
- Responsible
- Enthusiastic

- Dedicated
- Committed
- Reliable
- Trustworthy
- Initiative
- Team player
- Organised
- Focused

It is also a good idea to think of occasions where you have initiated projects or ideas at work, which have gone on to achieve results.

There now follows a sample response to this question. Once you have read it, use the template on the following page to create your own, based on your own individual situation:

"My strong points are that I am focused, professional, flexible, enthusiastic and dedicated. For example, whilst working for my current employer I was successful in achieving my annual appraisal sales target with 4 months to spare. I like to ensure that I maintain a healthy balance between my personal and professional life. This helps me to maintain a high level of performance at work.

I recently embarked on a Level 2 Civil Enforcement Officer course with the City and Guilds which I am now halfway through. I decided to take on this training in order to prepare myself for applying for this new role. I am an active person and enjoy visiting the gym 4 times a week which I believe will help me to perform the role of CEO competently and professionally. Some of my other hobbies include art, walking and cooking.

I am a caring person and when I have the spare time I try to get involved in community events in my local town. I recently ran a half marathon raising £450 for a local charity. Overall I would say that I am a reliable, a strong communicator, resilient, self-conscious and hard-working person who always looks for ways to improve."

SAMPLE INTERVIEW QUESTION - What can you tell us about the role of a Civil Enforcement Officer?

It goes without saying that you must have a thorough understanding of the role of a Civil Enforcement Officer. This is a guaranteed question at the interview. In order to answer it properly please refer to both the person specification and also the job description.

SAMPLE RESPONSE - What can you tell us about the role of a Civil Enforcement Officer?

"I understand that the role involves a high level of responsibility, concentration and lone working.

To begin with I will be responsible for carrying out designated patrols of car parks and streets that come within the Council's jurisdiction. I will need to check pay and display machines in car parks and on-street in accordance with the manufacturer's instructions. If I find that a machine is not functioning properly, I will need to remedy the malfunction or report the fault to the maintenance contractor and Senior Car Park Inspector immediately. In addition to these duties I will also be required to re-stock pay and display machines with tickets and collect cash where necessary.

I will also be primarily responsible for ensuring vehicles parked in the car parks are parked in compliance with the Parking Places Orders and that vehicles parked on-street are in compliance with the Traffic Orders. If any vehicles do not comply then I will need to issue a Penalty Charge Notice. Other duties will include assisting in the good order of car parks and maintain reserved spaces for coaches, etc., report on defective, damaged or misleading signs, or other matters requiring attention from Council departments and which may invalidate the issue of a Penalty Charge Notice."

TEMPLATE FOR QUESTION – What can you tell us about the role of a Civil Enforcement Officer?

SAMPLE INTERVIEW QUESTION – What skills do you possess that you think would be an asset to our team?

When responding to questions of this nature, try to match your skills with the skills that are required of a Civil Enforcement Officer. On most Local Authority websites, you will be able to see the type of person they are looking to employ, usually in the recruitment section or the Parking Services section.

An example of this would be:

'We are currently seeking to recruit a Parking Enforcement Officer. Your role is to ensure effective enforcement of the

Parking Regulations and the smooth flow of vehicular traffic and assist with additional duties when requested. You must be able to exercise sound judgement and decisions. A flexible attitude to working hours and the introduction of new processes are a must. Excellent customer care skills and communication skills are also required.

Just by looking at the Local Authorities website you should be able to obtain some clues as to the type of person they are seeking to employ. Try to think of the skills that are required to perform the role you are applying for and include them in your response.

The following is a sample response to the question. Once you have read it, take the time to construct your own response using the template provided.

SAMPLE RESPONSE - What skills do you possess that you think would be an asset to our team?

"I am a very conscientious person who takes the time to learn and develop new skills correctly. I have vast experience working in a customer-focused environment and fully understand that customer satisfaction is important in the role of a Civil Enforcement Officer, especially as I will be representing the Local Authority. Without the public there would be no service, so it is important that every member of the Local Authority team works towards providing a high level of service.

I believe I have the skills, knowledge and experience to do this. I am a very good team player and can always be relied upon to carry out my role to the highest of standards. I am a flexible person and understand that there is a need to be available at short notice to cover duties if required, especially at weekends and in the evenings. In addition to these skills and attributes, I am a very good communicator. I have experience of having to communicate to customers in my previous role and believe that this would be an asset in the role of a Civil Enforcement Officer. I am highly safety conscious and have a health and safety qualification to my name. Therefore, I can be relied upon to perform all procedures relevant to the codes of conduct and will not put myself or others in any danger whatsoever. Finally, I am very good at learning new skills which means that I will work hard to pass all of my exams and training if I am successful in becoming a Civil Enforcement Officer."

TEMPLATE FOR QUESTION – What skills do you possess that you think would be an asset to our team?

SAMPLE INTERVIEW QUESTION - Can you tell us about a situation when you have had to work under pressure?

The role of a Civil Enforcement Officer will sometimes involve a requirement to work under pressure. Therefore, the assessors want to know that you have the ability to perform in such an environment.

If you have experience of working under pressure then you are far more likely to succeed as a CEO.

When responding to a question of this nature, try to provide an actual example of where you have achieved a task whilst being under pressure. Questions of this nature are sometimes included in the application form, so try to use a different example for the interview.

I have provided you with a sample response to this question. Once you have read it, take the time to construct your own response based on your own individual experiences and knowledge using the template provided.

SAMPLE RESPONSE - Can you tell us about a situation when you have had to work under pressure?

"Yes, I can. In my current job as car mechanic for a well- known company, I was presented with a difficult and pressurised situation. A member of the team had made a mistake and had fitted a number of wrong components to a car. The car in question was due to be picked up at 2pm and the customer had stated how important it was that his car was ready on time because he had an important meeting to attend.

We only had two hours in which to resolve the issue and I volunteered to be the one who would carry out the work on the car. The problem was that we had three other customers in the workshop waiting for their cars too, so I was the only person who could be spared at that particular time. I worked solidly for the next two hours making sure that I meticulously carried out each task in line with our operating procedures.

Even though I didn't finish the car until 2.10pm, I managed to achieve a very difficult task under pressurised conditions whilst keeping strictly to procedures and regulations."

TEMPLATE FOR QUESTION – Can you tell us about a situation when you had to work under pressure?

SAMPLE INTERVIEW QUESTION- Can you tell me about a time when you have worked as part of a team to achieve a goal?

Having the ability to work as part of a team is very important to the role of a Civil Enforcement Officer. Although there will be lots of lone working, you will be working as part of the wider Parking Services team which form part of the Local Authority. As a CEO you will be working alongside, and communicating with, other CEO's, Police Community Support Officer's, Wardens and other key members of the Council. The recruitment staff will want to be certain that you can work effectively as part of a team, which is why you may be asked questions that relate to your team working experience. There now follows a sample response to this question. Once you have read it, take time to construct your own response using the template provided.

SAMPLE RESPONSE - Can you tell me about a time when you have worked as part of a team to achieve a goal?

"Yes, I can. I like to keep fit and healthy and as part of this aim I play football for a local Sunday team. We had worked very hard to get to the cup final and we were faced with playing a very good opposition team who had recently won the league title. After only ten minutes of play, one of our players was sent off and we conceded a penalty as a result. Being one goal down and 80 minutes left to play we were faced with a mountain to climb. However, we all remembered our training and worked very hard in order to prevent any more goals being scored. Due to playing with ten players, I had to switch positions and play as a defender, something that I am not used to. The team worked brilliantly to hold off any further opposing goals and after 60 minutes we managed to get an equaliser. The game went to penalties in the end and we managed to win the cup. I believe I am an excellent team player and can always be relied upon to work as an effective team member at all times. I understand that being an effective team member is very important if the Local Authority is to provide a high level of service to the public. However, above all of this, effective teamwork is essential in order to maintain the high safety standards that are set."

TEMPLATE FOR QUESTION – Can you tell me about a time when you have worked as part of a team to achieve a goal?

SAMPLE INTERVIEW QUESTION - Can you provide us with an example of a project you have had to complete and the obstacles you had to overcome?

Having the ability to complete tasks and projects successfully demonstrates that you have the ability to complete your Civil Enforcement Officer training. Many people give up on things in life and fail to achieve their goals. The recruitment staff need to be convinced that you are going to complete all training successfully and, if you can provide evidence of where you have already done this, then this will go in your favour.

When responding to this type of question, try to think of a difficult, drawn out task that you achieved despite a number of obstacles that were in your way. You may choose to use examples from your work life or even from some recent academic work that you have carried out. Take a look at the following sample question before using the template provided to construct your own response based on your own experiences.

SAMPLE RESPONSE - Can you provide us with an example of a project you have had to complete and the obstacles you had to overcome?

"Yes I can. I recently successfully completed a NEBOSH course (National Examination Board in Occupational Safety and Health) via distance learning. The course took two years to complete in total and I had to carry out all studying in my own time whilst holding down my current job.

The biggest obstacle I had to overcome was finding the time to complete the work to the high standard that I wanted to achieve. I decided to manage my time effectively and I allocated two hours every evening of the working week in which to complete the work required. I found the time management difficult but I stuck with it and I was determined to complete the course.

In the end I achieved very good results and I very much enjoyed the experience and challenge. I have a determined nature and I have the ability to concentrate for long periods of time when required. I can be relied upon to finish projects to a high standard.

TEMPLATE FOR QUESTION – Can you provide us with an example of a project you have had to complete and the obstacles you had to overcome?

SAMPLE INTERVIEW QUESTION – What are your weaknesses and what do you need to work on?

This is a classic interview question and can be quite difficult to answer for many people.

Those people who say they have no weaknesses are not telling the truth. We all have areas that we can improve on, but you need to be careful what you disclose when responding to this type of question.

For example, if you tell the panel that you are an awful time keeper you might as well leave the interview there and then! They will admire your honesty, but the role of Civil Enforcement Officer requires people who are punctual and are not going to be late for work.

The best way to prepare for this type of question is to write down all of your weaknesses. Once you have done that, pick one that you can turn into a positive. Take a look at the sample response that follows and see how we have turned the weakness around to our advantage.

Once you have read the response, use a blank sheet of paper to prepare your own response based on your own circumstances.

SAMPLE RESPONSE - What are your weaknesses and what do you need to work on?

'That's a difficult question to answer but I am aware of a weakness that I have. I tend to set myself very high standards both personally and professionally.

The problem is, I sometimes expect it from other people, too. For example, I find it difficult to accept it when people are late for an appointment that we have agreed.

In those situations, I need to learn to let it go over my head and just accept that everybody is different.'

KEY AREAS TO CONSIDER:

- Be honest, but don't talk about any weaknesses you may have that are in relation to the job description.

- Turn your weakness into a positive.

- Say that you are working on your weakness.

- If you really cannot think of a weakness, tell them about one that you used to have.

TEMPLATE FOR QUESTION – What are your weaknesses and what do you need to work on?

SAMPLE INTERVIEW QUESTION - Describe a situation at work where you have had to be flexible.

Part of the Civil Enforcement Officer's role is to be flexible. This means that you are flexible in terms of the working day and also your ability to work some weekends.

In order for the Parking Services team to operate an outstanding service to the public, it needs people who do not want to work a normal 9 – 5 job. You may have to work some weekends, start or early and work late, or even work Bank Holidays. Are you flexible enough to do this?

Read the sample response we have provided before using a blank sheet of paper to create your own response.

SAMPLE RESPONSE - Describe a situation at work where you have had to be flexible.

'Whilst working in my current role as a hairdresser, I was asked by my employer to work late every Saturday evening. The reason for this was that a number of clients could only make appointments between 6pm and 8pm on Saturday evenings. Although I usually go out on a Saturday night, I decided to agree to the additional hours. The salon was doing well and was beginning to get a very good reputation. I wanted to help the salon provide a high level of service to its customers and understood that if I didn't work late on those evenings they would lose the custom.

Fortunately, 2 months on, another member of the team has volunteered to help me cover the Saturday evenings, so I now only have to work every other Saturday.

I fully understand that Civil Enforcement Officers need to be flexible in terms of their shifts and unsociable working hours. My personal life would allow for this and I believe it is a small sacrifice to pay for such a rewarding career. I can be relied upon to be flexible when required.'

KEY AREAS TO CONSIDER:

- Demonstrate that your personal circumstances allow for flexibility.

- Provide an example where you have gone out of your way to help your employer.

- Tell the interview panel that you understand how important flexible working is to the role of a CEO.

TEMPLATE FOR QUESTION – Describe a situation at work where you have had to be flexible.

SAMPLE INTERVIEW QUESTION – What is the best example of customer service that you have come across?

The majority of Local Authorities pride themselves on their high level of service. However, some are better than others.

This type of question is designed to see how high your standards are, in relation to customer service. Those people who have a great deal of experience in a customer-focused environment will be able to answer this question with relative ease. However, those who have little experience in this area will need to spend more time preparing their response.

Try to think of an occasion when you have witnessed an excellent piece of customer service and show that you learned from it. If you are very confident, then you may have an occasion when you, yourself, provided that service. Whatever response you provide, make sure it is unique and stands out.

There now follows a sample response that relates to an individual who went that extra mile to make certain the customer was happy.

Once you have read it, use a blank sheet of paper to create your own.

SAMPLE RESPONSE - What is the best example of customer service that you have come across?

'Whilst working as a shop assistant in my current role, a member of the public came in to complain to the manager about a pair of football shoes that he had bought for his son's birthday. When his son came to open the present on the morning of his birthday, he noticed that one of the football boots was a larger size than the other. He was supposed to be playing football with his friends that morning and wanted to wear his new boots. However, due to the shop's mistake, this was not possible.

Naturally, the boy was very upset. The manager of the shop was excellent in her approach to dealing with situation. She remained calm throughout and listened to the gentleman very carefully, showing complete empathy for his son's situation. This immediately defused any potential confrontation. She then told him how sorry she was for the mistake that had happened, and that she would feel exactly the same if it was her own son who it had happened to. She then told the gentleman that she would refund the money in full and give his son a new pair of football boots to the same value as the previous pair. The man was delighted with her offer. Not only that, she then offered to give the man a further discount of 10% on any future purchase, due to the added inconvenience that was caused by him having to return to the shop to sort out the problem. I learned a lot from the way my manager dealt with this situation. She used exceptional communication skills and remained calm throughout.

She then went the extra mile to make the gentleman's journey back to the shop a worthwhile one.

The potential for losing a customer was averted by her actions and I feel sure the man would return to our shop again.'

KEY AREAS TO CONSIDER:

- Use an example where somebody has gone the extra mile.

- Remember that part of the role of a Civil Enforcement Officer is to provide a high level of customer service.

- Tell them what you learned from the experience.

TEMPLATE FOR QUESTION – What is the best example of customer service that you have come across?

SAMPLE INTERVIEW QUESTION - Have you ever lost your temper?

This is a great interview question and is not easy to answer. All of us have lost our temper at some point, but you need to be careful as to how much you disclose.

Part of the role of a Civil Enforcement Officer is to remain calm under pressure and you need to demonstrate this in your response. They do not want to employ people who lose their temper at the slightest hint of confrontation from members of the public who are on the receiving end of a parking fine. It is during these times that you will need to use your skills to defuse the conflict. Having said all of that, it is also not your job to accept any form of abuse from members of the public and you will need to know when report such incidents to your line manager or the police.

The question is designed to see how honest you are, and whether you are a naturally aggressive person. It is ok to lose your temper at times during your personal life, but it is not welcome as a CEO. Resilient and assertive, yes; aggressive, no.

How would it look if you saw a Civil Enforcement Officer losing his/her temper in the street? It would be very embarrassing and unprofessional!

Take a look at the sample response that follows before taking the time to construct your own.

SAMPLE RESPONSE - Have you ever lost your temper?

'In the whole I am a calm person and do not become aggressive or confrontational.

Whilst it is only natural to be annoyed with people from time to time, I see no point in losing my temper. It is just wasted energy.

I understand that Civil Enforcement Officers cannot lose their temper with members of the public or anyone for that matter; it would be highly unprofessional. I appreciate that it must be frustrating at times dealing with difficult and irate members of the public, but the way to resolve issues is to remain calm, professional and resilient. It is also very important to follow your training and organisational guidelines.'

KEY AREAS TO CONSIDER:

- Try to use 'non-confrontational' words and phrases during your response – patience, calm, understanding, etc.

- Demonstrate your understanding of the CEO's role and the importance of remaining calm and professional.

TEMPLATE FOR QUESTION – Have you ever lost your temper?

SAMPLE INTERVIEW QUESTION - Tell us about your hobbies and what you get up to in your spare time?

Whilst this is an easy question to answer you should consider how some of your hobbies may come across. Good hobbies to have are sports, fitness, walking, traveling, languages and culture and music.

SAMPLE RESPONSE - Tell us about your hobbies and what you get up to in your spare time?

'I am quite a grounded person but I do have a few hobbies. I love keeping fit and active and I attend the gym a few times a week. I also enjoy traveling and love being away from home. I think it makes you appreciate your home life when you do return after being away from home for a few weeks. When I travel I enjoy learning about the different cultures and I am also currently learning a new language. When I am not at work I enjoy spending time with my family who are very supportive of my aspiration to become a Civil Enforcement Officer.'

KEY AREAS TO CONSIDER:

- A hobby can say a lot about you.

- Think carefully about how your hobbies will portray you to the interview panel.

- Hobbies that involve fitness and health are positive.

TEMPLATE FOR QUESTION – Tell us about your hobbies and what you get up to in your spare time?

SAMPLE INTERVIEW QUESTION - Tell us how you would deal with a complaint from a member of the public?

Dealing with and resolving a complaint is all part and parcel of the CEO role. You should have a thorough knowledge and understanding of how to deal with them.

In any industry or profession where a customer or member of the public is complaining, there are a number of key areas that the complainant is concerned with:

- They want someone to **listen** to their complaint.
- They want someone to **understand** why they are complaining.
- They want someone to **sort out** their complaint as soon as possible.
- They would like an **apology**.
- They want someone to **explain** what has gone wrong.

Civil Enforcement Officers are required to deal with complaints in an efficient and effective manner, whilst following their training, guidelines and procedures. When dealing with complaints in any form, you will need to follow an action plan. This action plan is explained in detail on the following pages. Whilst I haven't provided you with a specific response to this question, the following information and guidance will help you to answer it sufficiently.

The plan follows a structured format and each area follows on systematically from the other. To begin with, you will listen to the complaint using effective verbal and nonverbal listening skills. The majority of people associate communication skills primarily with the spoken word. However, these cover a number of areas. Having the ability to actively listen is a key factor to resolving the complaint successfully. Take a look at the stages of dealing with complaints successfully.

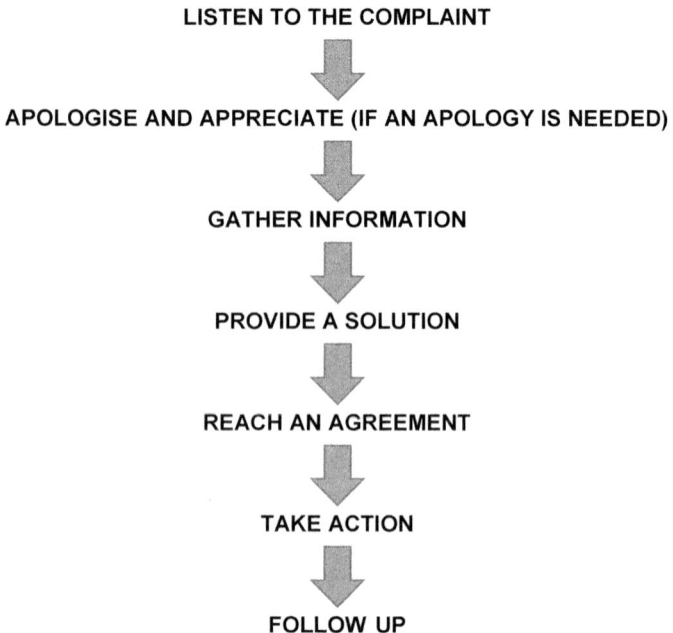

LISTEN TO THE COMPLAINT

APOLOGISE AND APPRECIATE (IF AN APOLOGY IS NEEDED)

GATHER INFORMATION

PROVIDE A SOLUTION

REACH AN AGREEMENT

TAKE ACTION

FOLLOW UP

SAMPLE INTERVIEW QUESTION - What are your strengths?

The most effective way to answer this question is to first of all read the job description and person specification for the job. Once you have done this you will have a good idea of what the main qualities of the role are. You should then answer the question by providing strengths that match the main qualities of the role. This will ensure that you get the highest scores possible for this question. To begin with let's take a look at some of the main qualities required to a Civil Enforcement Officer:

- Effective communicator.
- Team worker.
- Flexible and approachable.
- Customer service orientated.
- Professional.
- Adaptable.
- Intuitive.

Now take a look at the following response to this question which perfectly matches these qualities.

SAMPLE RESPONSE - What are your strengths?

'To begin with, I am an excellent communicator and I am able to deal with people from diverse backgrounds comfortable and proficiently. I really enjoy working with other people and I have a happy disposition and a caring nature. Another of my strengths is that I have a flexible approach to work and life in general and I am always highly professional in a work-related situation. Finally, I am adaptable, conscientious, highly organised and can be relied upon to work very hard for any organisation.'

KEY AREAS TO CONSIDER:

- Get a copy of the job description and match the key qualities in your response.

- Use positive keywords and phrases in your response that match the main qualities required in the role.

TEMPLATE FOR QUESTION – What are your strengths?

SAMPLE INTERVIEW QUESTION - Do you have any experience of working as a team member?

The ability to work effectively in a team is an extremely important aspect of the role. Not only will you be liaising with other members of the Parking Services team, you will also be required to communicate and work with members of the police and other services. Therefore, it is important that you can demonstrate you have the ability to work as an effective team member.

When responding to this type of question, try to think of occasions when you have been part of a team and achieved a common goal. It is important that you give EVIDENCE of where you have already worked as part of a team in a work situation.

Maybe you are already involved in team sports playing hockey or football? You may also find that you have experience of working as a team member through work. If you have none or very little experience of working as a team member then try to get some before you apply to become a CEO. After all, teamwork is an important aspect of the role.

Now take a look at the following sample response.

SAMPLE RESPONSE - Do you have any experience of working as a team member?

'Yes I have many years' experience of working in a team environment. To begin with, I have been playing hockey for my local team for the last 3 years. We worked really hard together improving our skills over the course of last season and we managed to win the league.

I am also very much involved in teamwork in my current job. I work as a nurse at the local hospital and in order for the ward to function correctly we must work effectively as a team. My job is to check all of the patients at the beginning of my shift and also make sure that we have enough medical supplies to last the duration. It is then my responsibility to inform the ward sister that the checks have been carried out. She will then obtain more supplies if we need them.

We have to work very closely together for many hours and we all pull together whenever the going gets tough. I enjoy working in a team environment and feel comfortable whilst working under pressure. I would have no problems working as part of a team in my role as Civil Enforcement Officer if I am successful.'

KEY AREAS TO CONIDER:

- It is important that you provide EVIDENCE of your ability to work as part of a team.

- Before you attend the interview have an understanding of what teamwork is, what it involves and the qualities each team member should possess.

TEMPLATE FOR QUESTION – Do you have any experience of working as a team member?

SAMPLE INTERVIEW QUESTION - Tell me about a time when you changed how you did something in response to feedback from someone else?

When working as a CEO you will need to have the ability to listen to, and respond to, feedback from senior members of the Parking Services Team. You should also possess the maturity to admit when you get things wrong and take steps to improve wherever possible. There are always new procedures to learn whilst working as a CEO and you will receive appraisals on a yearly basis from your superiors.

Here is a good response to this question.

SAMPLE RESPONSE - Tell me about a time when you changed how you did something in response to feedback from someone else?

'During my last appraisal, my line manager identified that I needed to improve in a specific area. I work as a call handler for a large independent communications company. Part of my role involves answering a specific number of calls per hour. If I do not reach my target then this does not allow the company to meet its standards. I found that I was falling behind on the number of calls answered and this was identified during the appraisal. I needed to develop my skills in the manner in which I handled the call. My line manager played back a number of recorded calls that I had dealt with and it was apparent that I was taking too long speaking to the customer about issues that were irrelevant to the call itself. Because I am conscientious and caring person I found myself asking the customer how they were and what kind of day they were having. I was spending too much time on delivering a high quality service to the customer as opposed to working through the call as fast as possible so that I could answer the next one.

Despite the customers being more than pleased with level of customer care, this approach was not helping the company and therefore I needed to change my approach. I immediately took on-board the comments of my line manager and also took up the offer of development and call handling training. After the training, which took two weeks to complete, I was meeting my targets with ease. This in turn helped the company to reach its call handling targets.'

KEY AREAS TO CONIDER:

- How you respond to feedback is very important. Try to give a good example where you improved following feedback in a work-related situation.

TEMPLATE FOR QUESTION – Tell me about a time when you changed how you did something in response to feedback from someone else?

SAMPLE INTERVIEW QUESTION - What do you understand about the term Health and Safety and who is responsible for it?

Health and Safety plays a very important part in the CEO's working day.

As a Civil Enforcement Officer you will be acutely aware of Health and Safety and how it affects you and your colleagues. Health and Safety is the responsibility of everybody at work. Health and Safety at work is governed by the Health and Safety at Work Act 1974 and the Management of Health and Safety at Work Regulations 1999. Whilst you may not need to know it for your interview, my advice would be to understand the term 'risk assessment' and what it means to your role.

The following is a sample response to this type of question.

SAMPLE RESPONSE - What do you understand about the term Health and Safety and who is responsible for it?

"Everybody is responsible for Health and Safety at work. Health and Safety is governed by the Health and safety at Work Act 1974 and the Management of Health and Safety at Work Regulations 1999. Civil Enforcement Officers are responsible for the safety of themselves and the safety of each other.

Health and Safety is all about staying safe and promoting good working practices. In the role of a CEO this means making sure that the clothing is worn when required, following rules and procedures, checking that equipment I use is serviceable and carrying out risk assessments when required. It also includes simple things like making sure I am aware of traffic and vehicles around me whilst walking on and working around the streets of my dedicated area."

TEMPLATE FOR QUESTION – What do you understand about the term Health and Safety and who is responsible for it?

SAMPLE INTERVIEW QUESTION - What do you think the important elements of communicating with different groups of people are?

A question based around your communication skills is likely to appear during the CEO interview. Remember that Civil Enforcement Officers have to be good communicators and be capable of working with people from every part of the community.

The following is a sample response to this question to help you structure your own.

SAMPLE RESPONSE - What do you think the important elements of communicating with different groups of people are?

"Effective communication skills are an integral part of the CEO role. One of the main elements is respect. Being respectful of people's backgrounds and trying to appreciate how they feel about things, particularly whilst working in the Local Authority and the community, is important so that good relationships can be built.

CEO's also need to be able to communicate effectively and accurately both verbally and also in writing. It is not good to record inaccurate details of a parking fine that has been issued as this will simply look unprofessional, create additional work for other members of the team and also render the parking fine invalid.

Listening effectively is also another important aspect of good communication. Listening to what people say and getting feedback is important so that improvements can be made.

When communicating it is vital that Civil Enforcement Officers create an approachable and positive image so that trust can be built. Asking questions is important too so that messages are relayed accurately."

TEMPLATE FOR QUESTION – What do you think the important elements of communicating with different groups of people are?

SAMPLE INTERVIEW QUESTION - Is there a standard approach used by Civil Enforcement Officer's?

This question is designed to assess whether or not you have carried out any research in relation to the role of becoming a Civil Enforcement Officer. CEO's will follow a standard approach when issuing Parking Charge Notices (PCN) and this guidance will come from the CEO handbook. I recommend you download a copy of the handbook online and study its content. You do not need to know the content inside out prior to interview, however, it is important to be aware of its existence and what information it contains.

SAMPLE RESPONSE - Is there a standard approach used by Civil Enforcement Officer's?

"Yes, the approach is defined in the Civil Enforcement Officer's Handbook. The local authority should produce a handbook for CEO's. This should be based on the training given to CEO's and could be used both as part of that training and as a guide to procedures for officers on duty. The handbook should explain the different types of parking contravention.

Many authorities that already have civil parking enforcement powers, and service providers, have handbooks which can be used as a model. An authority could prepare a handbook alongside the specification for tenderers wishing to provide CEO services. Alternatively, an authority could require the contractor to provide a suitable handbook. The authority should check that the instructions in any handbook produced by a contractor comply with the law.

For London Boroughs, the Civil Enforcement Officers (CEO) handbook has been devised after general consultation with all Borough's to provide a standard approach to issuing Penalty Charge Notices (PCNs). Parking contraventions are dealt with by issuing a Penalty Charge Notice and, in appropriate circumstances, by clamping or removing the vehicle to a pound. The handbook provides guidance which has general relevance throughout a specific area. It is accepted that there will be local variations in policy and these will be a matter for each London Borough.

CEO's will be instructed on how to deal with local variations. The handbook is intended as a reference document for use on-street or in the office. It describes the contraventions, their codes and details of information to be recorded in each case in order to prove that the contravention took place."

TEMPLATE FOR QUESTION – Is there a standard approach used by Civil Enforcement Officer's?

FURTHER RECOMMENDED INTERVIEW QUESTIONS TO PREPARE FOR

The previous sample interview questions are a great place to start your preparation. Below, I have provided you with a few more to help you during your preparation.

Q. What type of work does the Parking Services Team carry out and how do we support Civil Enforcement Officers?

Q. Describe a typical working day of Civil Enforcement Officer?

Q. What are the different areas covered by CEO's in the County area you are applying for?

Q. How would you defuse a confrontational situation with an irate member of the public?

Q. What type of training would you undergo as a CEO if you are to be successful?

Q. What is the name and location of all the car parks within the area you are applying to become a CEO in?

Q. You are on patrol as a Civil Enforcement Officer and a member of the public approaches you and asks you how they can apply for a residents parking permit. What do you tell them?

Q. What are the main qualities required to become a CEO?

Asking questions at the end of the interview

Once the interview is over you may be given the opportunity to ask the panel a couple of questions yourself. It is bad practice to not have any questions prepared, so make sure you have two ready in preparation. Personally, I would avoid asking any more than two or three questions. You should remember that the interview panel are busy and that they have other people to interview. I advise that you ask insightful questions that put you across in a positive manner. Here are three great questions to ask the panel:

Q1. **Whilst I am waiting to find out if I am successful or not, is there any further literature of information you can recommend I study to further enhance my knowledge of the company?**

This question is great because it shows that you are keen, eager and hungry for more information.

Q2. What is the Parking Services Team approach to the training and development of its new staff?

This is a good question because it shows that you understand how important training and development is.

At the end of the interview

Once the interview is over you may be given the opportunity to say a final few words. If this is the case, try saying something like:

'Thank you for inviting me along to the interview today, I have thoroughly enjoyed it. I wanted to say that if I am successful I can assure you that I will provide a level of service and will work hard to achieve the high standards that the Parking Services Team sets. Thank you for your time.'

CHAPTER 8

How to get Civil Enforcement Officer fit – bonus section

HOW TO GET CIVIL ENFORCEMENT OFFICER FIT – BONUS SECTION

Welcome to your FREE 'How to get Civil Enforcement Officer fit' information guide. Within this guide you will find some very useful tips for helping you get, and stay, CEO fit.

Whilst there is no actual physical fitness test for becoming a Civil Enforcement Officer, it is important that you prove to the recruitment staff that you are fit to perform the role. Within this guide I have provided a number of exercises for everybody. In truth, perhaps the best form of exercise to prepare for the role of CEO is walking. As a CEO you will walk approximately 7 miles day!

I recommend that you do not spend hours in the gym lifting heavy weights but rather aim for a varied and diverse fitness programme that cover exercises such as swimming, rowing, jogging, brisk walking and light weight work.

In addition to getting fit, keep an eye on your diet and try to eat healthy foods whilst drinking plenty of water. It will all go a long way to helping you improve your general well-being and concentration levels.

PLANNING YOUR WORKOUTS IN ORDER TO GET FIT

Most people who embark on a fitness regime in January have given it up by February. The reason why most people give up their fitness regime so soon is mainly due to a lack of proper preparation. You will recall that throughout the duration of this guide the word preparation has been integral, and the same word applies when preparing to achieve a good level of fitness. Preparation is key to your success and it is essential that you plan your workouts effectively.

Read on for some great ways to not only be physically fit for the demands of the CEO role, but to also stay fully fit all year round!

Get an assessment before you start training

The first step is to get a fitness test at the gym, weigh yourself and run your fastest mile. Once you have done all three of these you should write down your results and keep them hidden away somewhere safe. After a month of following your new fitness regime, do all 3 tests again and check your results against the previous months. This is a great way to monitor your performance and progress and it will also keep you motivated and focused on your goals.

Keep a check on what you eat and drink

Make sure you write down everything you eat and drink for a whole week. You must include tea, water, milk, biscuits and anything and everything that you digest. You will soon begin to realise how much you are eating and you will notice areas in which you can make some changes. For example, if you are taking sugar with your tea then why not try reducing it or giving it up all together. If you do then you will soon notice the difference.

It is important that you start to look for opportunities to improve your fitness and well-being right from the offset. These areas are what I call 'easy wins'.

You don't need to go to a gym in order to get fit

Walking is one of the best exercises you can do as part of your preparation for the role of CEO. Whilst it shouldn't be the only form of exercise you carry out, it will go a long way to improving your focus and general wellbeing. Now, when I say 'walking' I don't mean a gentle stroll, I mean 'brisk' walking. Try walking at a fast pace for 30 minutes every day for a 7 day period. Then see how you feel at the end of the 7 day period. I guarantee you'll begin to feel a lot healthier and fitter. Brisk walking is also a fantastic way to lose weight too, if you think you need to.

There are some more great exercises contained within this guide and most of them can be carried out without the need to attend a gym.

One step at a time

Only you will know how fit you are. I advise that you first of all write down the areas that you believe or feel you need to improve on. For example, if you feel that you want to work on your upper body strength then pick out exercises from this guide that will work on that area for you.

The key to making improvements is to do it gradually, and at one step at a time. Try to set yourself small goals. If you think you need to lose two stone in weight then focus on losing a few pounds at a time. For example, during the first month aim to lose 6 pounds only. Once you have achieved this then again aim to lose 6 pounds over the next month, and so on and so forth. The more realistic your goal, the more likely you are to achieve it. One of the biggest problems that people encounter when starting a fitness regime is they become bored quickly. This then leads to a lack of motivation and desire, and soon the fitness programme stops.

Change your exercise routine often. Instead of walking try jogging. Instead of jogging try cycling with the odd day of swimming. Keep your workouts varied and interesting to ensure that you stay focused and motivated.

STRETCHING

How many people stretch before carrying out any form of exercise? Very few people is the correct answer. Not only is it irresponsible but it is also placing yourself at high risk from injury. Before we commence with the exercises we will take a look at a few warm up stretches. Make sure you stretch fully before carrying out any exercises. You want your career as a Civil Enforcement Officer to be a long one and that means looking after yourself, including stretching! It is also very important to check with your GP that you are medically fit to carry out any form of physical exercise.

The warm-up calf stretch

To perform this stretch effectively you should first of all start off by facing a wall whilst standing upright. Your right foot should be close to the wall and your right knee bent. Now place your hands flat against the wall and at a height that is level with your shoulders. Stretch your left leg far out behind you without lifting your toes and heel off the floor, and lean towards the wall.

Once you have performed this stretch for 25 seconds switch legs and carry out the same procedure for the left leg. As with all exercises contained within this guide, stop if you feel any pain or discomfort.

Stretching the shoulder muscles

To begin with, stand with your feet slightly apart and with your knees only slightly bent. Now hold your arms right out in front of you and with your palms facing away from you with your fingers pointing skywards. Now place your right palm on the back of your left hand and use it to push the left hand further away from you. If you are performing this exercise correctly then you will feel the muscles in your shoulder stretching. Hold for 10 seconds before switching sides.

Stretching the quad muscles (front of the thigh)

Before you carry out any form of brisk walking or running then it is imperative that you stretch your leg muscles. To begin with, stand with your right hand pressed against the back of a wall or firm surface. Bend your left knee and bring your left heel up to your bottom whilst grasping your foot with your left hand. Your back should be straight and your shoulders, hips and knees should all be in line at all times during the exercise. Hold for 25 seconds before switching legs.

Stretching the hamstring muscles (back of the thigh)

It is very easy to injure your hamstring muscles as a CEO. Imagine all of the walking that you'll do during your career. Therefore, you must get into the routine of stretching out the hamstring muscles before every training session.

To perform this exercise correctly, stand up straight and place your right foot onto a table or other firm surface so that your leg is almost parallel to the floor. Keep your left leg straight and your foot at a right angle to your leg. Start to slowly move your hands down your right leg towards your ankle until you feel tension on the underside of your thigh. When you feel this tension you know that you are starting to stretch the hamstring muscles. Hold for 25 seconds before switching legs.

We have only covered a small number of stretching exercises within this section; however, it is crucial that you stretch out fully in all areas before carrying out any of the following exercises. Remember to obtain professional advice before carrying out type of exercise.

RUNNING

One of the great ways to greatly improve your overall fitness levels is to embark on a structured running programme. You do not need to run at a fast pace or even run for long distances, in order to gain massively from this type of exercise.

Before I joined the Fire Service I spent a few years in the Royal Navy. I applied to join the Navy when I was 16 and I made it through the selection process with ease until I reached the medical. During the medical the doctor told me that I was overweight and that I had to lose a stone before they would accept me. To be honest, I was heart-broken. I couldn't believe it, especially after all that hard work I had put in preparing for the tests and the interview! Anyway, as soon as I arrived back home from the medical I started out on a structured running programme that would see me lose the stone in weight within only 4 weeks! The following running programme is very similar to one I used all those years ago.

Before I provide you with the running programme however, take a read of the following important running tips.

Tips for running

• As with any exercise you should consult a doctor before taking part to make sure that you are medically fit.

• It is certainly worth investing in a pair of comfortable running shoes that serve the purpose for your intended training programme. Your local sports shop will be able to advise you on the types that are best for you. You don't have to spend a fortune to buy a good pair of running shoes.

• It is a good idea to invest in a 'high visibility' jacket or coat so that you can be seen by fast moving traffic if you intend to run on or near the road.

• Make sure you carry out at least 5 whole minutes of stretching exercises not only before but also after your running programme. This can help to prevent injury.

• Whilst you shouldn't run on a full stomach, it is also not good to run on an empty one either. A great food to eat approximately 30 minutes before a run is a banana. This is great for giving you energy.

• Drink plenty of water throughout the day. Try to drink at least 1.5 litres each day in total. This will keep you hydrated and help to prevent muscle cramp.

• Don't overdo it. If you feel any pain or discomfort then stop and seek medical advice.

RUNNING PROGRAMME WEEK 1

DAY 1

- Run a total of 3 miles only at a steady pace.
- If you cannot manage 3 miles then try the following:
- Walk at a brisk pace for half a mile or approximately 10 minutes.
  Then
- Run for 1 mile or 8 minutes.
  Then
- Walk for another half a mile or approximately 10 minutes.
  Then
- Run for 1.5 miles or 12 minutes.

Walking at a brisk pace is probably the most effective way to lose weight if you need to. It is possible to burn the same amount of calories if you walk the same distance as if you were running.

When walking at a 'brisk' pace it is recommended that you walk as fast as is comfortably possible without breaking into a run or slow jog.

RUNNING PROGRAMME WEEK 1

DAY 2

- Walk for 2 miles or approximately 20 minutes at a brisk pace.
  Then
- Run for 2 miles or 14 minutes.

DAY 3

- Repeat DAY ONE.

DAY 4

- Walk at a brisk pace for 0.5 miles or approximately 7 minutes.
  Then
- Run for 3 miles or 20 minutes.

DAY 5

- Repeat day one.

DAY 6 AND DAY 7

- Rest days. No exercise.

RUNNING PROGRAMME WEEK 2

DAY 1

Run for 4 miles or 25 minutes.

DAY 2

- Run a total of 3 miles at a steady pace.
  If you cannot manage 3 miles then try the following:
- Walk at a brisk pace for half a mile or approximately
  10 minutes.
  Then
- Run for 1 mile or 8 minutes.
  Then
- Walk for another half a mile or approximately 10 minutes.
  Then
- Run for 1.5 miles or 12 minutes.

RUNNING PROGRAMME WEEK 2

DAY 3

- Rest day. No exercise.

DAY 4

- Run for 5 miles or 35 - 40 minutes.

DAY 5

- Run for 3 miles or 20 minutes.
  Then
- Walk at a brisk pace for 2 miles or approximately 20 minutes.

DAY 6

- Run for 5 miles or 35 – 45 minutes.

DAY 7

- Rest day. No exercise.

Once you have completed the second week running programme, use the 3rd week to perform different types of exercises, such as cycling and swimming. During week 4 you can then commence the 2 week running programme again. You'll be amazed at how easier it is the second time around!

When preparing for the CEO selection process, use your exercise time as a break from your studies. For example, if you have practising numerical reasoning tests for an hour, why not take a break and go running? When you return from your run you can then concentrate on your studies feeling refreshed

Now that I've provided you with a structured running programme to follow, there really are no excuses. So, get out there and start running! I'll now provide you with a number of key targeted exercises that will allow you to get really fit for your duties as a CEO.

EXERCISES THAT WILL IMPROVE YOUR OVERALL PHYSICAL FITNESS

Press-ups

Whilst running is a great way to improve your overall fitness, you may also want to carry out exercises that improve your upper body strength. The great thing about press-ups is that you don't have to attend a gym to perform them. However, you must ensure that you can do them correctly as injury can occur. You only need to spend just 5 minutes every day on press-ups, possibly after you go running or even before if you prefer. If you are not used to doing press-ups then start slowly and aim to carry out at least 10.

Even if you struggle to do just 10, you will soon find that after a few days practice at these you will be up to 20+.

Step 1 - To begin with, lie on a mat or even surface. Your hands should be shoulder width apart & fully extend the arms.

Step 2 - Gradually lower your body until the elbows reach 90°. Do not rush the movement as you may cause injury.

Step 3 - Once your elbows reach 90° slowly return to the starting position with your arms fully extended.

The press up action should be a continuous movement with no rest. However, it is important that the exercise is as smooth as possible and there should be no jolting or sudden movements. Try to complete as many press ups as possible and always keep a record of how many you do. This will keep your focus and also maintain your motivation levels. Did you know that the world record for non-stop press-ups is currently 10,507 set in 1980!

WARNING – Ensure you take advice from a competent fitness trainer in relation to the correct execution of press-up exercises and other exercises contained within this guide.

Sit-ups

Sit ups are great for building the core stomach muscles. At the commencement of the exercise lie flat on your back with your knees bent at a 45° angle and with your feet together. Your hands can either be crossed on your chest, by your sides, or cupped behind your ears as indicated in the diagram below.

Without moving your lower body, curl your upper torso upwards and in towards your knees, until your shoulder blades are as high off the ground as possible. As you reach the highest point, tighten your abdominal muscles for a brief second. This will allow you to get the most out of the exercise. Now slowly start to lower yourself back to the starting position. You should be aiming to work up to at least 50 effective sit-ups every day. You will be amazed at how quickly this can be achieved and you will begin to notice your stomach muscles developing.

Sit ups are a great way of improving your all-round fitness and therefore should not be neglected.

Pull-ups

Pull ups are another great way for building the core upper body muscle groups. The unfortunate thing about this type of exercise is you will probably need to attend a gym in order to carry them out. Having said that, there are a number of different types of 'pull up bars' available to buy on the market that can easily and safely be fitted to a doorway at home. If you choose to purchase one of these items make sure that it conforms to the relevant safety standards first.

Lateral pull-ups are very effective at increasing upper body strength. If you have access to a gymnasium then these can be practised on a 'lateral pull-down' machine. It is advised that you consult your gym member of staff to ask about these exercises.

Pull ups should be performed by grasping firmly a sturdy and solid bar. Before you grasp the bar make sure it is safe. Your hands should be roughly shoulder width apart. Straighten your arms so that your body hangs loose. You will feel your lateral muscles and biceps stretching as you hang in the air. This is the starting position for the lateral pull up exercise.

Next, pull yourself upwards to the point where your chest is almost touching the bar and your chin is actually over the bar. Whilst pulling upwards, focus on keeping your body straight without any arching or swinging as this can result in injury. Once your chin is over the bar, you can lower yourself back down to the initial starting position. Repeat the exercise 10 times.

Squats (these work the legs and bottom)

Squats are a great exercise for working the leg muscles. They are the perfect exercise in your preparation for the role of a Civil Enforcement Officer.

At the commencement of the exercise, stand up straight with your arms at your sides. Concentrate on keeping your feet shoulder-width apart and your head up. Do not look downwards at any point during the exercise. You will see from the diagram above that the person has their lower back slightly arched. They are also holding light weights which can add to the intensity of the exercise.

Now start to very slowly bend your knees while pushing your rear out as though you are about to sit down on a chair. Keep lowering yourself down until your thighs reach pas the 90° point. Make sure your weight is on your heels so that your knees do not extend over your toes. At this point you may wish to tighten your thighs and buttocks to intensify the exercise.

As you come back up to a standing position, push down through your heels which will allow you to maintain your balance. Repeat the exercise 15 to 20 times.

Lunges (these work the thighs and bottom)

You will have noticed throughout this section of the guide that I have been providing you with simple, yet highly effective exercises that can be carried out at home. The lunge exercise is another great addition to the range of exercises that require no attendance at the gym. Simply because they concentrate on building the necessary core muscles to perform the demanding tasks of the job.

To begin with, stand with your back straight and your feet together (you may hold light hand weights if you wish to add some intensity to the exercise).

Next, take a big step forward as illustrated in the above diagram making sure you inhale as go and landing with the heel first. Bend the front knee no more than 90 degrees so as to avoid injury. Keep your back straight and lower the back knee as close to the floor as possible. Your front knee should be lined up over your ankle and your back thigh should be in line with your back.

To complete the exercise, exhale and push down against your front heel, squeezing your buttocks tight as you rise back to a starting position.

Try to repeat the exercise 15 to 20 times before switching sides.

Lateral raises (these work the shoulder muscles)

My advice is that you perform lateral raises as part of your training programme as they are a fantastic exercise for building and developing the shoulder muscle groups.

Take a dumbbell in each hand and hold them by the sides of your body with the palms facing inward.

Stand or sit with your feet shoulder-width apart, knees slightly bent. Do not lean backwards as you could cause injury to your back. Raise your arms up and out to the sides until they are parallel to the ground, then lower them back down carefully. Repeat the exercise 15 to 20 times.

The above exercises will allow you to improve on your upper and lower body strength.

ALTERNATIVES EXERCISES

Swimming

Apart from press-ups, lateral raises and the other exercises I have provided you with, another fantastic way to improve your upper body and overall fitness is to go swimming. If you have access to a swimming pool, and you can swim, then this is a brilliant way to improve your fitness.

If you are not a great swimmer you can start off with short distances and gradually build up your swimming strength and stamina. Breaststroke is sufficient for building good upper body strength providing you put the effort into swimming an effective number of lengths. You may wish to alternate your running programme with the odd day of swimming. If you can swim 10 lengths of a 25-metre pool initially then this is a good base to start from. You will soon find that you can increase this number easily providing that you carry on swimming every week. Try running to your local swimming pool if it is not too far away, swimming 20 lengths of breaststroke, and then running back home.

This is a great way to combine your fitness activity and prevent yourself from becoming bored of your training programme.

The multi stage fitness test or bleep test

A great way to build endurance and stamina is by training with the Multi Stage fitness test or bleep test as it is otherwise called.

The multi stage fitness test is used by sports coaches and trainers to estimate an athlete's VO2 Max (maximum oxygen uptake). The test is especially useful for players of sports like football, hockey or rugby. The test itself can be obtained through various websites on the internet and it is great for building your endurance and stamina levels. You can obtain a copy of the Bleep Test from the website **www.how2become.com.**

TIPS FOR STAYING WITH YOUR WORKOUT

The hardest part of your training programme will be sticking with it. In this final section of your fitness guide I will provide some useful golden rules that will enable you to maintain your motivational levels. In order to stay with your workout for longer, try following these simple rules:

Golden rule number one - Work out often

Aim to train three to five times each and every week.

Each training session should last between 20 minutes to a maximum of an hour. The quality of training is important so don't go for heavy weights but instead go for a lighter weight with a better technique. On days when you are feeling energetic, take advantage of this opportunity and do more!

Within this guide I have deliberately provided you with a number of 'simple to perform' exercises. In between your study sessions try carrying out these exercises at home or get yourself out on road running or cycling. Use your study 'down time' effectively and wisely.

Golden rule number two - Mix up your exercises

Your exercise programme should include some elements of cardiovascular (aerobics, running, brisk walking and cycling), resistance training (weights or own body exercises such as press-ups and sit ups) and, finally, flexibility (stretching). Make sure that you always warm up and warm down.

If you are a member of a gym then consider taking up a class such as Pilates. This form of exercise class will teach you how to build core training into your exercise principles, and show you how to hit your abdominals in ways that are not possible with conventional sit-ups. If you are a member of a gym then a fantastic 'all round' exercise that I strongly recommend is rowing. Rowing will hit every major muscle group in your body and it is also perfect for improving your stamina levels and cardiovascular fitness.

Golden rule number three - Eat a healthy and balanced diet

It is vitally important that you eat the right fuel to give you the energy to train to your full potential. Don't fill your body with rubbish and then expect to train well. Think about what you are eating and drinking, including the quantities, and keep a record of what you are digesting. You will become stronger and fitter more quickly if you eat little amounts of nutritious foods at short intervals.

Golden rule number four - Get help

Try working with a personal trainer. They will ensure that you work hard and will help you to achieve your goals. If you cannot afford a personal trainer then try training with someone else. The mere fact that they are there at your side will add an element of competition to your training sessions!

A consultation with a professional nutritionist will also help you improve your eating habits and establish your individual food needs.

Golden rule number five - Fitness is for life

Working out and eating correctly are not short-term projects. They are things that should be as natural to us as brushing our teeth.

Make fitness a permanent part of your life by following these tips, and you'll lead a better and more fulfilling life!

Good luck and work hard to improve your weak areas.

A FEW FINAL WORDS

You have now reached the end of the guide and no doubt you will be ready to start preparing for the Civil Enforcement Officer selection process. Just before you go off and start on your preparation, consider the following.

Throughout my life I have always found a number of common factors in those people who achieve success. These are as follows:

1. They believe in themselves.

The first factor is self-belief. Regardless of what anyone tells you, you can become a CEO. Just like any job of this nature, you have to be prepared to work hard in order to be successful. Make sure you have the self-belief to pass the selection process and fill your mind with positive thoughts.

2. They prepare fully.

The second factor is preparation. When I joined the Fire Service I was amazed at how many people said to me 'you're lucky to get a job in the Fire Service'. I didn't bother responding to comments like this because I knew 100% that there was no luck involved in my success. It was down solely to the amount of preparation I had put in during the weeks and months leading up to the selection process. Those people who achieve in life prepare fully for every eventuality and that is what you must do when you apply to become a Civil Enforcement Officer. Work very hard and especially concentrate on your weak areas.

3. They persevere.

Perseverance is my favourite word. Everybody comes across obstacles or setbacks in their life, but is what you do about those setbacks that is important. If I fail at something, then I want to know 'why' I've failed. This allows me to improve for next time and I always know that if I keep improving and trying, success will follow. Apply this same method of thinking when you apply to become a CEO.

4. They are self-motivated.

How much do you want this job? Do you want it, or do you really want it? For the weeks and months leading up to CEO selection, be motivated as best you can and always keep your fitness levels up as this will serve to increase your levels of motivation.

Work hard, stay focused and be what you want...

Richard McMunn

how2become

Visit www.how2become.com to find more titles and courses that will help you to pass the Civil Enforcement Officer selection process, including:

- How to pass job interview books and DVD's.

- CEO books, DVDs and courses.

- Psychometric testing books and CD's.

www.How2Become.com

Printed in Great Britain
by Amazon